BREAK Your *Self-Help* ADDICTION

Praise for the Book

"*Break your Self-Help Addiction* shares a method that dives straight into the core of the issue transforming old patterns and beliefs. Brian's expertise, intuitive leadership and communication skills make him an excellent transformational mentor. His book is beyond the extraordinary."

—**Maria Clara Castaneda**, www.mariaclaracastaneda.com

"I LOVE this book, Brian! Well put together and I love what you're up to…helping people raise their level of consciousness and vibration so they can experience more of whatever it is they want to experience! Thank you for being a light!"

—**Bryan Dulaney**, www.perfectfunnelsystem.com

"Very powerful book that will transform the lives of the readers, unless they are just totally unopen to change and happy stuck in their misery! Thanks for sharing your experience-based wisdom and guidance!"

—**Willie Crawford**, www.williecrawford.com

"In this inspiring book, Brian first shares his story of how he transformed his life from a living Hell to a grace-filled Heaven, and then outlines powerful tools and distinctions to help us all do the same and become Conscious Creators of every aspect of our lives! He is so humorous, genius and generous with his mind-blowing wisdom and packs so much incredible value into this book. Thank you, Brian, for helping us to remember our Infinite Identity, and sharing tools that help us to access, embody and live that experience now and ever more!"

—**Jade Rajbir Kaur**, www.theradiantlotus.org

"This is one of the greatest awakening books I have ever read and the answers I have been searching for are contained within. It is quite simply a brilliant look at our paradigms and why other 'self help' doesn't create lasting successes. Please, you owe it to your soul to get inspired with this book. Brian is genius, controversial and outspoken and finally I discovered someone who tells it like it is—not from theory, but from years of self-exploration and self-discovery. A must read! Put down ALL other books—this IS the one you deserve!"

—**Tim Bennett**, www.directorofwow.com

Praise for Brian's Work

"I've sought out and worked with the best of the best. Brian is the best I have ever seen at helping people get to the core of their problems and solve them."

—**Blake R. Goodwin**, CEO of VideoOptimize

"I've been involved with personal development and self-help for the last 25 years. I'm an NLP trainer and seminar leader. I've done many, many top-level programs, including Core Transformation and Core Energetics, most of Tony Robbins' programs and more. I'm also a Hypnotist and have worked as a Hypnotism Instructor. I have tried, applied and even taught much of what is out there in the self-help and personal development world. In 15 minutes, Brian was able to help me dissolve a deep issue I had dealt with for nearly my entire life. His is the fastest, most powerful and fun transformational work I have ever experienced."

—**Joan Tremblay**, Corporate Coach and Trainer

"As the most confirmed anti-woo-woo guy on the planet just a couple of years ago, I have seen the light. Brian's work changed everything— watch what happens to your business, your bank account, your relationships… everything."

—**Jack Humphrey**, Author of *Bending The Web* and *The Ultimate Guide to Google Plus*

"Brian completely changed my life. My income, my relationships, my confidence. It is amazing."

—**Carie Jackson**, Arbonne Independent Rep

"I've invested over $50,000 on personal development work—so I was skeptical. I got more out of a one-hour session with Brian than out of all of those years and dollars of investment. I highly recommend him."

—**Bryan Dulaney**, Co-Founder, CMO at 7 Figure Sales Training

"The list of things Brian has helped me with—and the speed of his work—is incredible. In less than an hour, the grief I carried from the passing of my first husband was gone. Completely gone. I had tried so many things, but his work is just amazing. Next, I had been on medication for Restless Leg Syndrome for over ten years. With Brian's 'magic,' I was able to drop the medication and do my own inner healing."

—**Pallavi Kapoor**, Natural Healing Oasis

"I can definitely say that Brian has a real gift, and has the ability to help you get that laser-focus. I'd say to work with him before he gets too well-known."

—**Tom Beal**, Chief Inspiration Officer at MakeTodayGreat.com

"My first experience with Brian created the biggest business breakthrough of my life. It all happened in 15 minutes. I joined his mentoring program and watched similar breakthroughs with person after person he touched. But I would never have believed that one session with him could lead to me releasing the Scoliosis I had for the previous 30 years. This is a literal miracle."

—**Erica Hooft**, Eigenaresse at LichtWesen Nederland
(The Netherlands)

"In my first experience with Brian, I experienced so much light. I reached a higher place than I've ever experienced. Now, five days later, I know that my essence is flowing back to me, I feel so much stronger, and still smiling from the inside."

—**Armona Livneh**, Hypnotherapist to the Stars

"Bottom line on Brian's work—it's pretty amazing stuff. I've been through tons of personal development over the years and never experienced anything like this before."

—**Harris Fellman**, Founder / President / CEO at Another Zero, LLC

"Brian's message is clear and I think his teachings will change the Self-Help Industry for ever! His New approach to Law of Attraction truly is Leading Edge Thinking! If you're looking for LASTING change in any area of your Life. Brian's webinar is for You!"

—**James Kirouac**, Quantum Healing Hypnosis Practitioner

"Even after decades as a coach, mentor and speaker, and helping thousands of people, I had a long-standing 'stuck' issue in my life. In just ONE experience with Brian, he completely shifted my energy and brought me through to a state of clarity and power…I wouldn't have believed it could be that easy if I hadn't experienced it for myself."

—**Lynn Pierce**, CEO & Founder at Ageless Lifestyle After 50.com

"Brian really helped me to see things in a new and powerful way. What surprised me the most is that after just one experience with him, my perceptions, and my interactions with others, shifted dramatically and it felt like I totally controlled the outcomes. It has brought me to a completely new level of income and happiness."

—**Willie Crawford**, Chief Executive Officer at Willie Crawford Marketing Tips

"What an amazing experience! I have already, in this one session with Brian, shifted some core beliefs that I hadn't even been completely aware of. I am looking forward to learning more of these simple, powerful tools in our coaching sessions to come."

—**Cynthia Tiano**, Conscious Relationship Mediator and Coach

"Incredible work! Within 15 minutes of finishing our session, a miracle manifested. Could it be this simple—the answer is YES. When you choose to be supported by Brian—you are re- minded and will re-member who you truly are."

—**Dr. David Gawain**, Naturopathic Healer

"As a Certified Master Life Coach, I seek out and work with the best. I joined Brian's Conscious Creators' Program. During the FIRST session, my mind was completely blown. He is the REAL DEAL. Life transformed."

—**Dena Sawyer**, CMLC

"After one session with Brian, I am no longer stuck. I would classify Brian as a genius at communication, most importantly the way we communicate with ourselves."

—**David Kinney**, President, The Kinney Group

"In just minutes Brian can change your life. I have had many encounters with Brian and, every time, I have discovered something new of who I am. If you want to be free of the false self that you think you are, Brian is the go-to."

—**Carol Ann Snyder**, Consultant at Mary & Martha

"I have attended far too many seminars that dealt with business, personal development and continuing education where the majority of it is 'filler' and a waste, both for the company and for the people in the field. I have to say I cannot remember when I ever came away with the knowledge that I have been seeking for oh so long! Most people in our industry are suffering from the lack of this crucial knowledge. As a result of Brian's gifts and ability to transform lives, I opted to join his 90 day mentoring program. 1 week in—and it is already more than I expected."

—**Dr. Richard Muccillo**, NMD

"In all of my life of personal development study, training and teaching, I have never encountered anything like Brian's work. It is amazing, powerful, mind-blowing."

—**Javier Rivera**, Author, Speaker

"I'm not into the "woo-woo" fluffy stuff and I was a bit skeptical. But somehow, Brian was able to help me, in one session, to find and release a major life issue that had been holding me back—that I didn't even know I had! Brian is THE guy who can help you, too."

—**Felicia Slattery**, Communications Expert

"I was pretty skeptical about the entire idea Brian presented. And then, amazingly, when he helped me with a few personal issues, my business immediately doubled. Amazing."

—**Jack Vidal**, Former VP Media at Moburst—Mobile Marketing

"Brian is an incredible mentor, trainer and teacher. Expect profound, life-changing results."

—**Tyler Hoff**, Entrepreneur and Co-creator at HempAware

"Wow, ONE session with Brian D. Ridgway, and I am blown away by how easily he was able to guide me to answers within myself, that have been holding me back from accepting love, joy & abundance in my personal & business life. Brian, thank you, and I am looking forward to your next webinar."

—**Stephanie Sterling**, Sterling International Marketing Group

"I've been studying self-development, motivation and sales for the last 30 plus years, and I've attended conferences, webinars, seminars, and bought books, DVDs, etc. learning material we don't get in a college or university. I just witnessed the future of Personal Development on a webinar with Brian D. Ridgway. On one free session, I let go of a massive hidden block. This is good stuff."

—**Roger Neumann**, Author, Sales Trainer, Speaker

BREAK
Your *Self-Help*
ADDICTION

The 5 Keys to Total Personal

Freedom

Brian D. Ridgway

NEW YORK

NASHVILLE • MELBOURNE • VANCOUVER

BREAK Your *Self-Help* ADDICTION
The 5 Keys to Total Personal *Freedom*

Published in New York, New York, by Morgan James Publishing in partnership with Difference Press. Morgan James is a trademark of Morgan James, LLC. www.MorganJamesPublishing.com

The Morgan James Speakers Group can bring authors to your live event. For more information or to book an event visit The Morgan James Speakers Group at www.TheMorganJamesSpeakersGroup.com.

ISBN 978-1-68350-445-0 paperback
ISBN 978-1-68350-166-4 eBook
Library of Congress Control Number: 2017901697

Cover Design by:
Rachel Lopez
www.r2cdesign.com

Interior Design by:
Bonnie Bushman
The Whole Caboodle Graphic Design

Author's photo courtesy of
Alannah Avelin
AlannahVision.com

In an effort to support local communities, raise awareness and funds, Morgan James Publishing donates a percentage of all book sales for the life of each book to Habitat for Humanity Peninsula and Greater Williamsburg.

Get involved today! Visit
www.MorganJamesBuilds.com

DISCLAIMER

Our modern world is filled with medical establishments which have given themselves "legal monopolistic authority" status. Those "quasi-legal" entities, all living in the first two paradigms, make it necessary for me to include this BS disclaimer:

Dedication

To my children, Brent, Johnathan,
Crystalin, Nathan, Sukhi, and Orion.
You are my greatest teachers.

Table of Contents

Introduction		**xxiv**
	Thank You for Picking Up This Book	xxiv
	The Miracle	xxviii
	GO DEEPER	xxx
	Consciously Creating Your Life	xxxi
Chapter 1	**My Story**	**1**
	Staying Stuck with My Spells	5
	My Business Success Was "BS"	8
	I Lost It All—Seven Times	9
	At Rock-Bottom—The Miracle	11
	The Universe Delivers—Instantly	15
	In Summary	17
	Secrets of a Conscious Creator: On Skepticism	18
	90-Day Skepticism-Elimination Experiment	20
	Two Questions	20
Chapter 2	**Make the Unconscious Conscious**	**22**
	Your True Identity	23
	Other Concepts Coming Up	24
	Secrets of a Conscious Creator: On the "Fear of Success"	25
	EXERCISE	26

Chapter 3	**Spells**	**28**
	The Reality of Spells	29
	GO DEEPER	30
	The Endless Loop of Spells	30
	How I Became "The Spellbreaker"	32
	GO DEEPER	33
	Secrets of a Conscious Creator: On Breaking Spells	33
	Secrets of a Conscious Creator: On Spellbreaks	34
	What We've Covered So Far	35
	5 Keys to Total Personal and Financial Freedom	36
Chapter 4	**The First Key: Shift Your Core Paradigm**	**37**
	What Creates the "Illusion of Problems"	37
	Hidden Core WHAT?	38
	We've Been All Wrong	41
	The Power of a CORE Paradigm Shift	44
	What Exactly Is a Paradigm and What Is *Your* Core Paradigm?	44
	The 4 "Lower" Paradigms	46
	The Level 5 Paradigm—Oneness	50
	GO DEEPER	52
	HOW We Learned These "Spells"	52
	GO DEEPER	56
	The Creation Myth (Or More Accurately, Subatomic Magic)	56
	Creation and Light	58
	Along Came Science…	60
	Jus' Blinkin' Lights	61
	Nothing "Matters"	62
	Secrets of a Conscious Creator: On The Universe	63
	Secrets of a Conscious Creator: What's the point?	66

Chapter 5	**The Second Key: Become Present and Centered in Your Power**	**67**
	The 5 Layer Breath Technique	68
	GO DEEPER	72
	The "Past Future Extraction" Technique	72
	GO DEEPER	74
	Secrets of a Conscious Creator: On Breathing	74
Chapter 6	**The Third Key: Focus on What You Want to Experience**	**76**
	The Outcome of Falling into Thought	77
	Focusing on What You Want to Experience	78
	Secrets of a Conscious Creator: On Focus	81
Chapter 7	**The Fourth Key: Clear the Past (Spellbreaks)**	**83**
	Honey, Where Did I Leave My Infinite Power?	84
	Why Spellbreaks Are Necessary	86
	1. Basic Self-Spellbreak	87
	2. The Complete Self-Spellbreak	89
	GO DEEPER	91
	3. Guided Spellbreaks	93
	GO DEEPER	93
Chapter 8	**The Fifth Key: Become the Master**	**95**
	Self-Love Is EVERYTHING	96
	Conscious Communication	96
	Adopting Blessed Perception	100
	Summary of the 5 Keys	102
	Secrets of a Conscious Creator: On Disease	103
	GO DEEPER	105
Chapter 9	**Don't F*** This One Up**	**106**
	A Periphery of Invisible Stop Signs	109
	The Old "You" Is "Against" You	110
	Your Environment Is "Against" You	111

	Your Mind is "Against" You	112
	Transformational Programs Are "Against" You	114
	Summary	114
	Secrets of a Conscious Creator: On Limitation	114
Chapter 10	**The Universe Is Waiting—Are You Coming?**	**116**
	Reconnecting with the Universe	116
	Joan's Story	117
	GO DEEPER	120
	Why I REALLY Wrote This Book	120
	GO DEEPER	123
	Acknowledgements	124
	About the Author	126
	About Level 5 Mentoring	128
	Let's Keep Talking	130

Preface

"If you knew Who walks beside you on the way that you have chosen, fear would be impossible."
—A Course in Miracles

I can't tell you the truth.

I can only tell you a truth. My truth.

When we go to the fringes of possibility, the word "truth" loses its meaning and relevance. To describe an <u>infinite</u>, <u>unlimited</u>, <u>eternal</u> energy is impossible. None of these three words are fully comprehensible to the human mind.

The word, "Infinite", itself points to being indefinable. As all spiritual traditions, wisdom sciences and thought systems have done, I will use word-symbols to explain the inexplicable.

An infinite universe can be "explained" in an infinite number of ways—and they will all be somewhat inaccurate. Some of the ways in which it has been explained to us are skewed in ways that block us from any possibility of seeing and accessing our true power.

Or, more accurately, and key to what you will discover in this book:

- our acceptance of those explanations and
- the things we think we "know" that arise out of that acceptance blocks us from seeing and accessing our true power.

In this book, you're going to experience miraculous information. I don't say this lightly.

This is information that has facilitated miracles in every area of life (body, health, business, wealth, relationships and more) for me and for thousands of people around the world.

This is life-changing, mind-bending, blending-the-most-advanced-quantum-physics-with-magic kind of stuff. Information that is aimed to take you beyond transformation, all of the way to liberation—or what I call "Total Personal Freedom".

The fact that you are here, on this page with me, tells me that you are willing to be open to seeing new light and experiencing more of your true power.

It is my intention to do everything in my power to help you. As a part of that intention, I'm making this much more than "just a book". Throughout the book, you'll find links to tools, resources and short, powerful video sequences that will bring the information to life—and help you to make the "transformation to liberation" *yours*.

If you keep a fully open mind, keeping curiosity alive, you are in for a wild ride—and the very high probability of a life full of miracles. (Oh, yeah, and the end of the self-help addiction.)

Before we jump in the stream together, I want to make something very clear for our mutual understanding and benefit:

In the Level 5 Paradigm, which you will learn about in these pages, there is really no such thing as "learning" or "teaching". The "weird cosmic truth" is that you *are* everything, and one with everything. And so, you already, technically, know everything.

I'm not a healer, a teacher, or a guru. I'm just a "reminder", here to remind you of what you already—and always—know:

There is a life waiting for you, brighter, more beautiful, and more full of light, love, joy and peace than you have ever allowed yourself to imagine or even dream.

Ready? Let's step into it...

Introduction

"In truth, there is no such thing as learning. You have it all inside you now. There is only the process of making the implicit explicit."
—Brian D. Ridgway

Thank You for Picking Up This Book

The simple fact that you are reading these first words tells me a few important things about you.

First, it tells me that you are seeking to live an amazing life—and, second, that you are committed to transforming your present life. And that you've already put time, effort and money into creating the life of your dreams. And, finally, that you still have one or more life-issues you would like to resolve.

Maybe parts of your life still flat-out suck.

Maybe your life is already great, and you are just seeking the next level of awesomeness.

Maybe, like me, you experienced a difficult, painful, abusive childhood, and you still experience the effects of it showing up in one or more areas of your life. Also, maybe like me, out of desperation, you've already tried many of the available solutions that promise to make life great—or even just to make it bearable.

Maybe, like me, you've spent a ton of money, time and energy on self-help, personal development work, and "spiritual" approaches, hoping to finally "find" your happiness, freedom, power and peace. Perhaps you've had some positive results, but the deep scars and pains remain.

Maybe, like many, you have accepted the possibility that you really *are* the one creating your life, and yet you're unclear on exactly how you've been doing it—and more importantly, on how to stop doing it "by default" and how to begin to do it intentionally.

Maybe, like me, you have spent a lot of time, energy and money on diving into the "deep stuff" and, finding yourself still stuck, you wonder if there might be something wrong with you—that maybe you are "broken" in some way.

Let me promise you this right now: You are NOT broken. And you ARE creating it all.

In the course of this book, I will make it clear, maybe more clear than you think is possible.

You'll discover:

- exactly how you are creating your life as it is
- how to stop doing it by default
- How to END the endless self-help loop of hope> purchase> disappointment> hope…

- and how to begin to consciously, intentionally create the *Body, Health, Business, Wealth, Relationships, World and Life of your dreams—how to step into Total Personal Freedom*

If you have felt confused, unclear, frustrated or disappointed in how to actually do this, I want you to know that I can relate and I understand. This book may just be the thing to finally end your search.

Before the breakthrough that set me free and that inspired me to write this book, my "previous life" was a train-wreck, a string of disasters, including multiple "failed" relationships, as well as the experience of making and losing a fortune (not once, but SEVEN times).

During much of my life, I felt a combination of severe anger and depression—and for several years, the thought of suicide was my ever-present companion.

I was certain that I needed help and was near-fanatical about pursuing any system or life-approach that offered hope of relief. My personal self-help focus was not a fun pursuit, a distraction or a luxury for me. It was a life or death necessity.

My journey into self-work started at a very young age. As a child, I heard about religion and the hope it offered for happiness. I was told that if I believed a certain way, and if I did x, y and z, life would get better. I listened, followed and did what "they" said. Life didn't get better.

In my late teens, I discovered self-help and personal development. Over the next 30 years, I invested well over $300,000 on any and every self-help book, seminar, course, program or tool that promised a miracle—or that even just offered to help me experience a life that worked. For many years, I literally devoted 20%-60% of my income into this pursuit.

Achieving the happy life and success promised by those shiny self-improvement programs was a worthy investment to me.

When all of that time, money and energy investment failed to turn my life around, I became desperate. This desperation led me to lay aside my skepticism of the more "woo woo", spiritual stuff out there.

I found it easy to understand why so many people become self-proclaimed "self-help junkies."

Maybe you can relate, too: I no longer trusted self-help to solve my problems—no longer believed the promises. But I literally could not see how to stop my self-help efforts.

I was desperate. And when next "promise" showed up, I felt hopeful again—invested again. I really applied myself to the information with trust and faith, again.

And when it inevitably "failed" (or when I did), I gave up again. And soon, there came the next shiny promise...

This led me to the next level of more "spiritually-focused" work. With desperation driving me to overcome my skepticism, I dove into every type of spiritual study, meditation approach, Law of Attraction training, coaching, belief-elimination course, seminar and program available.

Some of those programs helped a bit here and there. To be clear, I'm not "criticizing" self-help work, and I am not "putting down" any self-help authors. There is a LOT of great stuff out there. However, the vast majority of it does NOT break the box. It only helps people to live in larger boxes. Most approaches offer very limited results, very much "short-term" results—or results ONLY for people who are mentally/emotionally very similar to the author or creator of that specific program or book.

Through my decades of study and practice, I picked up a lot of *information*.

I experienced a lot of *fascination*.

I experienced some degree of *transformation*.

What nobody told me is that those are all distractions from what I really wanted, which was *liberation*. (If you are open, you will find the keys to the experience of liberation in this book.)

I like to joke that I became the World's Most Knowledgeable Positive Thinker, and yet, under it all, I had the sense of being a total and complete failure. Despite my best efforts, and despite tens of thousands of hours of studying self-help systems, my life just seemed to be in a miserable, endless, downward spiral.

After 30 years of near-fanatical devotion to my self-help junkie lifestyle, my life was worse than ever.

On top of my worsening life, and my continued experience of violated trust in the experts and "gurus", I was becoming ever-more confused by all of the conflicting information and systems of thought!

My failures in life were compounded by the fact that I couldn't even make self-help work! I often thought, "That stuff seems to work for everybody else, but there is something SO deeply flawed in me, that I can't even get self-help right!" The painful questions, "What is wrong with me? Am I so f*** up that even self-help can't help me?", were always buzzing in my mind. And my "extreme successes" in a few specific areas of life (more about that in the next chapter) actually caused me to feel worse, as I felt like a superficial fraud on top of it all.

And so, after more than $300,000 of financial investment, tens of thousands of hours of study and dedication, and over 30 years of self-help junkie-dom, I ended up homeless, hopeless, desperate, and suicidal.

The Miracle

And then in early 2011, I experienced an intense, profound, life-changing awakening.

A literal miracle.

In a FLASH, everything made sense. Thirty years of self-help work all came together in ONE inner explosion and I went from suicidal to emotionally free in seconds. Even better, this inner shift catapulted me from homeless in Van Nuys, CA—to a free all-expense-paid cruise in the Bahamas in 8 days—to living my dream in Hawaii in 67 days!

Miracles and awesomeness began to happen for me almost effortlessly. After that instantaneous shift from misery to grace, I was able to transform my suffering in hell into an amazing heaven-on-earth of Infinite Possibilities.

I went from the *idea* of Infinite Possibilities to *knowing and experiencing the deep reality of* Infinite Possibilities.

Since that miraculous moment, I've been able to help thousands of people all over the world take significant, often miraculous steps into the world of Infinite Possibilities. The huge majority of those people had already "tried everything" and by the time they found me, were deeply discouraged and skeptical.

So, if *you* feel skeptical right now, that is totally understandable. Don't worry. The fact that you're reading this tells me that, in all probability, you are ready to move from the conceptual to the experiential, and towards your own ultimate breakthrough.

You'll probably be encouraged to know that I've been able to help billionaires, high-level executives and professionals, people for whom "all of that Law of Attraction stuff" seems like fairy tales—and I've been able to help long-time spiritually-inclined people who "know it" but have never really been able to translate it into consistent personal experience.

And like my client Melissa says, "Many of the great authors, teachers and speakers were able to help me to see and get the idea of the Oneness and Infinite Possibilities. One session with Brian and within minutes, I was EXPERIENCING it."

Pause now for a moment. Check in with yourself. Close your eyes. Take a deep breath, and ask, "Am I ready?"

Did you get a clear, "yes"?

If so, here's exciting news:

In this book, you'll find the missing keys to living consistently in Infinite Possibilities.

I'll share the essential parts of my own story, and I'll also share the insights I received in that profound, Key Awakening Experience that changed everything for me. (After helping so many people around the world, and watching their miraculous breakthroughs, I know that sharing those two things alone are enough to inspire you towards your own Miracle Moment.)

But we won't stop there. I'm also going to share many of the Core Transformational Tools I've developed, tested and proven to assist you in expanding your "transformation to liberation" and keep it expanding for the rest of your life.

It's by applying these Core Transformational Tools that my clients, people from all over the world, have been able to shed their blockages and get "un-stuck" and IMMEDIATELY have unexplainably awesome things happen in their lives.

One of my clients, Lynn, expressed her experience with me this way: "Even after helping thousands of women around the world to transform their lives, especially around money, I still had blockages and issues with it. In one hour with Brian, it was gone. Right after the session, I felt the difference, and I got two speaking invitations seemingly 'out of the blue.' I wouldn't have believed it if I hadn't experienced it for myself."

When you get used to living in infinite possibility, these kind of results just become the norm. And it will begin for you before you even finish the book!

In order to get there like Lynn did, you have to take a step back and look at your "Universal Orientation".

GO DEEPER

Let's do a very short and very simple—yet powerful—exercise to jump-start your results, right now.

Go to **www.BreakYourSelfHelpAddiction.com/universal-orientation** and download the Universal Orientation Assessment. Make sure you have a pen and paper, and follow the steps. You'll find that you will have a profound realization of yourself and of the world you live in.

This simple process will make the book 100,000 times more valuable for you.

IMPORTANT: If you skim past this step (as you have may have skimmed over other things in the past), you're not going to get everything that you're here for. You've made the investment in this book. Please love yourself enough to take this step and get everything you can from your investment.

Consciously Creating Your Life

One of the Core Themes of my work, and of this book, is the idea of moving from "unconscious creation by default" to "Accessing and Intentionally Focusing Infinite Energy into the Conscious Creation of the life you want to experience". (Conscious Creation)

As I said earlier, the fact that you are reading this book tells me that you already know—or you suspect—that you <u>are</u> creating your life. In all probability, you also have the idea that you've been creating it largely unconsciously or, at best, semi-consciously.

In this book, I'm going to extensively, explicitly, and completely show you how to begin to *consciously create* the body, health, business, wealth, relationships, life and world of your dreams. I'm going to show you how to do that in every area of your life—with absolute clarity.

I'm also going to show you how to:

- Access more of your highest energies
- Use them to dissolve everything else that you've already created
- Learn to masterfully direct those energies into the creation of everything you want

Best of all, I'll also show you how to use those energies to dissolve limitations, in the moment, as they show up to block you from the life of your dreams. (This will make a lot more sense by the time you finish the next chapter—which is where are going right now.)

I'm about to tell you a story. Let's go…

Chapter 1

My Story

"Until you make the unconscious conscious, it will direct the events of your life and you will call it fate."
—Carl Jung

I have a very unusual gift.

For 46 years, it was my curse, a source of extreme pain and misery for me.

Today, many of my clients call it a miracle. I'll let you decide what it is for you.

Since 2 or 3 years of age, I've had the ability to simply look at a person for a few seconds, listen to their words, and know *exactly* how they are holding themselves back from what they want.

It's like I have a strange "mirror" in my awareness that allows me to see down into their mind and soul, to see exactly what is blocking them from accessing their highest resources—their Highest Being.

As a child, I didn't have words for it. No one around me could understand it.

I had no wisdom or understanding of how to intelligently use it, and so, until the age of 46, when I had my "Miracle Moment" (more about that in the next chapter) it was a curse. Let me tell you what I mean:

Even from early childhood, my love for people was overwhelming. I saw their pain and "stuckness", and I saw their "Infinite Truth", and I felt deeply and intensely compelled to help.

So, I immediately launched into telling them exactly how they were holding themselves back and how to get free.

Nearly everyone I did this "for", was either "freaked out", offended, or both.

Today, thankfully, I have a filter in place, and I am able to use this gift only when someone asks for it.

With this understanding of my "gift", let me tell you the whole story…

I was born in Columbus, Ohio, in 1964, and experienced a pretty rough childhood.

My dad was a very angry, 6-foot-4 redheaded man of Irish/English ancestry who had just gotten out of the military. He believed that life (for everyone) was the hellish life he had lived, and I'm sure he wanted to protect me from that. Based on the conclusions he reached as a result of the severe abuse he endured, he felt that he had to "beat me into" the shape that he "knew" would be "best for me" and that would make him "look good" as a father.

I was hit, beaten, ridiculed, and called names every day of my childhood. I lived in a state of ever-present fear—often panic—every day for the first 16 years of my life. I dreaded the evenings, knowing that after I heard his tires in the driveway, it was a matter of minutes before I received my "necessary" punishment for the day's events.

I always knew my mother loved me, and I know she always did her best, but she was not able to prevent him from hurting me. This added to my pain, fear and lack of trust in life and in my own safety.

From my parents I ended up getting the first of what I call— my "spells."

I will talk more about "spells" in a later chapter, but for now, I'll just mention that a "spell" is a mental/emotional/psychological state where one's behavior is quite literally "dictated" to them by the programming of a traumatic life incident—forming a "spell".

When under one or more spells, (I propose, and will show, that we are all under thousands of them) a person finds herself chronically, habitually behaving in less-than-conscious ways in one or more areas of life.

She finds herself consistently reacting to "triggers" which are hidden from her sight.

This creates a chronic situation in which the person finds unpleasant experiences repeating in her life, and feels helpless to change them or to overcome her reactions.

When the spell has intense emotion connected to it, it can cause us to experience "irrationally intense" emotion (out of proportion to the triggering event) every time the trigger is touched.

A spell that has intense emotion attached **and is associated with a wide-reaching area of life** (something that touches many areas of life, such as money, "love", the opposite sex, etc.) can create the circumstance where we are so often triggered—and to such an emotionally intense extent—that we appear "crazy" to others (and to ourselves). We can be literally unable to function in these areas—and, worse, we find ourselves unable to understand it, let alone explain it to others.

Just about every day for the first 16 years of my life, my "spells" were pretty much beaten into me with intense emotional and mental violence. Some of those "spells" were:

- I'm a bad boy
- I'm stupid
- Life is hard
- Bad boys don't deserve; therefore I don't deserve; therefore I can't have it (this leads to a very toxic and very destructive induction); if I DO get what I want, I will "pay"
- Dad can't be trusted; therefore men can't be trusted
- Mom can't keep me safe; therefore women can't be trusted
- I'm not safe
- I'm unlovable; therefore, if love comes, it will leave—painfully
- Love is unreliable
- When I use my gift, I get hurt even worse
- I'm ugly
- I'm worthless

So the mantra that I carried around for about the first 40 years of my life was that I am a "stupid, ugly, worthless piece of s***." That is, literally, what I was programmed to believe about myself, and for many decades, I did.

And my results "proved it" to me.

You might imagine that I was in pain. It was much worse than that.

Before we take the next step, I want to tell you the most insidious and devastating aspect of spells:

As I said a moment ago, when our spells are "taken on" in situations which include intense emotion, they get driven all of the way beyond our "mental body", beyond our "emotional body" and all of the way into our physical and energetic bodies.

How might this happen? There are three doorways:

1. Mental Trauma—Severe mental abuse, criticism, ridicule, etc.
2. Emotional Trauma—Being yelled at, or suffering severe criticism or abuse by someone we are very close to, such as a parent or sibling, "losing" someone through divorce or death, etc.
3. Physical Trauma—Being hit, punished, or slapped, by another person—or injured in any way

The most intense spells contain combinations of these. One of the most devastating combinations is physical abuse, by a parent, with intense mental and emotional "attack" or criticism.

When emotionally-impactful spells are taken on, they can trigger such intensely-irrational responses in us, so frequently, and with such intensity, that it leads people around us to think we are crazy or unstable. And, they are right. In those spell-charged areas, we are crazy and unstable.

Fortunately, I'm going to show you several ways to dissolve the roots of those traumas, probably in a way that goes much deeper than anything you have experienced before—or even imagined.

If you've been suffering from spells, or suspect you have, the answer is in the coming pages.

Staying Stuck with My Spells

Because I had constantly been told and shown how stupid I was, I became a fanatic about learning. I was fighting to not be stupid and to prove how brilliant I was. At four, I could read at a very high comprehension level. Throughout childhood, I pulled off some impressive "feats of smartness". I was still stuck "knowing" I was stupid.

Throughout my childhood, my "gift" (my ability to see down the core of "life-issues" and "core solutions" in others) grew and expanded. I was always, without exception, able to solve these issues for others. But my lack of wisdom in applying it caused my gift to be perceived as a flaw or problem in *me*. This made all of my other issues even more painful.

I got into religion, specifically Christianity, as a very young kid. I lived it, as best I could, for many, many years. I followed everything I understood to the best of my ability. Multiple churches and multiple denominations later, I had experienced lots of love, lots of learning and lots of insights; but my core issues never changed.

I got into Buddhism as a very young man. I was fanatical about studying and investigating the wisdom of Buddhism, and studying and practicing various types of meditation, but my core spells literally held me prisoner in my mind. My "failure" at meditation added to my perception of being "f*** up" and "broken beyond repair". Life still sucked.

In my twenties and thirties, I got into Hinduism and the Vedas. I was blown away by the depth, wisdom and brilliance of this fascinating science/religion. I received massive insights and illuminations… and my life was still a miserable nightmare… compounded by the fact that I was beginning to see that I was running out of options.

By this time, my gift had blossomed into a powerful, nearly magical ability. Nearly everyone I met was blown away by my ability. I helped a lot of people overcome a lot of issues. But, still, my lack of wisdom—my lack of knowing when to turn it off, or to "shut up" caused my greatest attribute to be the very thing that ran off the people I loved most.

With renewed fire from growing desperation, I dove into ever-"deeper" stuff: Dianetics, Scientology, "clearing methods" and a lot of different spiritual and emotional work; and I still stayed stuck.

There was no one there to explain this to me, but the truth was that those core issues of my life didn't change because I was still operating in a limited paradigm (more about this in a moment), informed and shaped by the sum of all of those spells.

After working as a professional musician through my late teens and twenties, I got into business in my early 30's. I wanted to make as much money as I could and to be as "successful" as I could possibly be. I continued buying books, programs, money/business/success courses, and seminars, as well as investing in coaching, and business/ life mentoring.

Despite my fanatical commitment and investment, I still stayed stuck.

I did, however, begin to make money. Soon, I was making a lot of it. And this made things even worse!

My "successes" in business were now activating my spells surrounding the ideas of success, failure, money and deservability. This created a severe conundrum: my every "success" brought more pain and "failure". I began to get the sense that I was digging myself a very deeeeeeeep, dark hole.

I began to notice that every time I started to experience any bit of forward motion, I was overwhelmed with feelings of:

- "I'm in trouble"—or "I'm about to be in trouble"
- "If this gets "better", the pain will follow swiftly"

As my life got worse, more and more out of control, I became more and more desperate. I was not going to give up. I couldn't! I did not want to continue living as I was—but I did not want to end my life. So I found myself diving into the "really far-out" stuff.

I got into Reiki, sound-healing, and all different types of energy work and manifestation work. I discovered Adamantine Energy teaching and different energy-and-light healing modalities. I created my own subliminal studio where I was making my own subliminal audio recordings, working with binaural brainwave beats, affirmations, incantations, chants…

All through this time, my own "gift" at helping others was becoming more and more fine-tuned, more and more powerful and effective. Everything I studied, investigated and applied made me even more effective at helping others. But I was never able to figure out how to use any of it to help myself.

So, I stayed focused on systems, tools and approaches "out there".

I got into all types of belief elimination and wisdom trainings, clearing and cleaning, auditing, anything to analyze and clear out my past trauma and spells. I hired energy workers, light-workers, shamans and all types of "healers". I learned more and more.

I had more insights.

Occasionally, I felt short-term relief.

My core issues stayed put and I stayed stuck, and ever-more hopeless.

To be clear, I am not "knocking" or devaluing any of those courses, programs or approaches. Every one of these tools, systems and products has value. A lot of people use them, and some have significant results. Most people do not. But as for me, like I said, I became the world's most positive thinker and boy, did I know a LOT about self-help, but yet I was still stuck. The core life issues did not change. My spells were dragging me deeper and deeper into a living hell.

My Business Success Was "BS"

During the early part of my adult life, in my sales and marketing career, I experienced what most people would call incredible business success. Well, at least "externally".

I created some very smart, innovative ideas, and I brought them to businesses ranging from "mom-and-pops", all the way up to multibillion-dollar corporations. I was able to generate about $161 million in total business revenues, in 70+ different industries, including $11 million that I did in personal sales. (All of that is documented.)

I noticed that my gift was becoming "miraculous" and more obvious. Nearly without exception, when I was consulting with a client, (business owners, CEOs, executives, etc.) a moment would come when they would feel compelled to share their deepest personal life issue with me. And without exception, I was able to reflect higher truth back to them.

I was gradually becoming aware that my business might be based more on "helping people" than "helping businesses".

The "biggest challenges" these people brought to me were literally effortless for me to shift. My gift was making my ability to make money easier and easier.

But in my own personal life, I was still totally stuck.

My life just continued to unravel, becoming worse and worse.

In fact, the more money I made, the more I suffered.

My "core spells" of "I don't deserve," "I'm a bad boy," "I can't have," "I'm not lovable," caused me to lose all the money that I had made—or more than I had made. And I did it over and over and over again.

I Lost It All—Seven Times

I had come from very, very humble beginnings. I *worked*. Hard. I probably had to work 10-20 times "harder" than most people have to—I had to strain against my "inner chains" (the chains of my spells) just to *function*. Through superhuman effort, and through my sales and marketing skills, and with the help of my gift, I was able to generate those significant amounts of money.

I made what was, to me, a fortune—and I lost it. And, thanks to my spells, I was able to pull off that "doom-loop" seven times in approximately an 8-year period.

During those years, I was becoming familiar with the Law of Attraction and other spiritual laws.

I began to see and accept that I was the one creating it all—that I, alone, was responsible. Many of the programs I studied proved to me that I, alone, was the cause. But none of them showed me exactly how to turn it around.

By this time, I had helped hundreds of people to overcome their issues. My insights gained from this unusual experience made it even more clear to me that the only issue those people were up against was "their own mindstuff". By simple logic, I knew that all of my problems were being caused by my own blind spots—my spells. But I just couldn't see how I was doing it.

I literally gave it everything I had. I prayed. I cried and cursed "God" and threatened to kill myself if She didn't help me. I visualized. I asked for guidance. I sought mentors and I invited those closest to me to please help me to see what I was missing.

I accepted that it was all me, but I could not see or figure out *how* it was me, *how* I was doing it.

I kept learning more. I kept applying what I learned. I modified my behavior and changed my language and "tried to think positively" and then it happened again.

And after the seventh time I lost everything, I nearly ended my life. The pain was unbearable. I had the ability to help anyone with any life issue, but seemed powerless to help myself.

If I could have afforded a gun, I probably would have stuck it in my mouth.

If it weren't for my kids, I would have definitely jumped in front of a subway train.

I knew that I alone had created this disaster. I KNEW that I was responsible, but didn't and couldn't understand how. I had tried everything, and nothing was working, and by this time, I was literally homeless, hopeless, desperate, stuck, and suicidal.

After 30+ years of self-help, tens of thousands of hours of self-work, hundreds of thousands invested in every program, course, book and seminar I could find, it had happened AGAIN!

And it had all led me to that moment. We had lost the Mercedes. Lost our home. Lost everything. I was married at that time, and was in a one-room hotel with my pregnant wife and two little ones. We had enough money for one last fast food meal, and one more night in that smoggy city. I had no idea what would or could happen next... It was, for all I could see, the end.

In that desperate place I looked back at all I had ever learned, back to all the religion, and all the self-help, and all the programs that I had ever been through, everything I had learned from applying my gift with others, and all of the spiritual truths and quantum physics insights I intellectually "knew".

This led to my "A-Ha" experience, my "miracle moment"...

At Rock-Bottom—The Miracle

For several months, I had been helping a friend with his business in Van Nuys, CA. Well, I was supposed to be helping with his business, but in truth, I was using my "gift" to help him with his personal life. I was barely making enough to keep my family off the streets in our dumpy little hotel room.

Despite the fact that it was our only source of income, I got the very clear guidance one morning to quit that project. It truly made no sense, but one valuable thing I had learned from all of my study and practice was to follow intuition and guidance—no matter what.

So I quit, left the office and went back to my dumpy little hotel room, wondering what the next disastrous occurrence would be.

The next morning, I received a very clear message to simply go down and sit by the hotel's microscopic swimming pool (literally not much bigger than a hot tub).

I thought, "I have no money. I have no options. I have no direction. I have enough money for one final night left here. After that, I can't even afford to move our meager belongings out of this motel room—and *then, we have nowhere to go!*

I guess if guidance says so, what the hell… I will just go down and sit by the pool."

All I had left was my intuition, and, as I said, I had learned to obey it. So I walked down to the pool and I sat there with my feet dangling on the edge.

Van Nuys, California. Smoggy, clogged, over-populated, gray city. At that time, I hated cities, hated smog and gray skies and vastly preferred nature and lots of green. I was in my own living hell.

I sat by this tiny little joke of a swimming pool at this dumpy motel, and the universe began to speak to me. Not audibly, not verbally, but the most clearly it ever had.

I felt the Universe say to me, "Think about all that quantum physics investigation you've done and everything you've learned. Think about everything you have discovered in all of those years of personal development, self-help, law of attraction, belief elimination…"

"Think about everything you have learned."

"Reflect on all of it."

"You know the Universe is an illusion."

"Are you REALLY in a hopeless situation?"

"Are you REALLY even here?"

In that moment I felt guidance—"Put your feet in the water," and so I put my feet in the water. The universe said, "Look at this," and I looked down at the pool. This little pool had the turquoise wrap lining the inside as most pools do. I looked down and realized that my feet were in turquoise water. I had this beautiful thought/feeling: "There is turquoise water in Hawaii, and in Cancun, and in the Bahamas, and in all the places I would infinitely rather be. My feet are in turquoise water right now." I smiled and felt a little bit of relief.

Then I looked up and I saw the blue sky. I thought, "Oh my God, a blue sky in gray Van Nuys! This is impossible." Then I realized that this was *the first time in months* that the sky had been blue. It had rained heavily for the previous three days and had stopped not long before I had walked down to the pool. So I looked up at this blue sky and I had this revelation: "Oh my God! That blue sky was there above the smog the whole time, wrapped around the entire planet. That same blue sky is above Cancun, and Hawaii, and the Bahamas, and all the places that I would much rather be. And here I am under that blue sky."

Then I felt the warm sun on my skin and I thought, "Oh my God! That same beautiful sun is shining above Mexico and above Hawaii, maybe at a different angle, but it is the same sun and it is warming my skin. I am sitting under this beautiful loving sun, under this beautiful blue sky, with my feet in turquoise water. Oh my God, I actually *am* in paradise—Now!"

For the first time in my entire life, I released all resistance to "what is".

I let go.

For the first time in my life, I "didn't know". I let go of my story.

My depression disappeared. And as my depression dissolved, I heard a bird whistle.

In one flash, everything I had ever learned about religion, spirituality, the law of attraction, personal development, self help, self improvement, the thousands of hours and dollars that I had invested all came and blasted through me in one flash! I saw the whole world and universe on a sub-subatomic level. I saw the Source of all, I felt the realization of myself as Source. I felt not just "connected" to the source, but I KNEW that I was and *am* the Source.

We are One.

All is One.

I felt, and knew, in that shining moment:

The source flows into me and through me

There is actually no physical universe here

There is only miraculous, sparkling energy blinking in and out of existence

There is no real continuity — the whole universe could instantaneously change into ANYTHING… it could become a marshmallow, and then a cup of hot cocoa, and then an onion, and then a universe, and then…

I realized, in that moment, one of the most crucial, critical, KEY truths that one must "get" in order to begin to break free from the "prison of the known", shared here for the second time:

**There is no continuity other than what
we think and believe that we know.**

This Key Revelation became one of the crucial core elements of my work. It is *important*, so please make a note of it. If it isn't 100% clear right now, trust me, it will be as we go through the following pages together.

Now, this series of insights and rush of revelations all occurred in maybe one or two seconds, but to me it seemed timeless. And I got the message, *direct from Source*, in total clarity:

"When you forget what you "know" about "What Is", and you accept, with peace, the perfect paradise you are in, no matter how it looks, you release all resistance to "What Is".

When you release all resistance to "What Is", only then can you change it. You make peace with where you are, and then, you can

instantly find yourself anywhere. <u>All</u> of your circumstances and life can change instantaneously."

I had moved—in a flash—from the *idea* of Infinite Possibilities to the *knowing* and *EXPERIENCE* of Infinite Possibilities.

For a long time, I had been learning that I was the one creating my hell, but I didn't know how.

Now, I knew how I had been creating it all.

And now, I knew exactly how to start creating exactly what I wanted to experience.

I sat there crying in bliss under an impossibly blue sky, now possible, under the beautiful sun, with my feet in turquoise water— knowing in every cell of my body that not only was I in paradise now, but I was also no longer a prisoner. I went from totally miserable, suicidal and stuck for 46 years of my life, to ecstatic and emotionally free in a matter of seconds.

That was my Miracle and my "A-ha moment."

I sat by the pool a while longer, crying and letting it all in. Then, guidance spoke again. I was guided back to the room to check my computer.

The Universe Delivers—Instantly

Recall that I had been working in sales and marketing. About a month earlier, I had seen a brilliant online business platform and had joined as an affiliate, hoping it might be my financial salvation. I was so impressed by the idea, I had created and posted a testimonial video about it online. And then, in my misery, I quickly forgot about it.

When I was guided to leave the pool to check my computer, I saw that I had just received an email from the CEO of the company behind the brilliant marketing platform!!! He mentioned that he had come across my video about his idea and he wanted me to call him immediately.

When he answered the phone, he said "Brian, I saw the video you had posted about my concept! I've been having a very difficult time expressing it and finding investors. You seem to understand it better than anyone on my team! I think you're the guy I've been looking for!

Would you please take over as the marketing director of my company, effective immediately?"

I was astounded. I had just left the pool and my Miracle Experience. I still had tears in my eyes.

I had enough money in my pocket to pay one more night and one more fast food meal for my family, and then nothing, no hope and no options—and then suddenly, I was being scooped up by the most exciting business idea I had ever seen...

He continued, "Oh, there's only one catch. I'm sure you have a lot going on. But I need you to be on a cruise representing my company. It's in eight days. It's all-expenses paid—and it's in the Bahamas. Can you possibly go?"

And eight days later I stepped on board the *Carnival Miracle*.

I was no longer stuck! This was the miracle that I had been waiting for my entire life. Within 67 days, I was able to move my family to Hawaii, a place where I literally could never have dreamed that I would be able to live.

What happened to me at that swimming pool is what can be called a Core Paradigm Shift. In that moment, I dissolved my "Primary Core Constraint" (more about that in the next chapter).

That one moment literally changed everything for me. It was the catalyst that broke several of my spells in ONE flash of power and insight.

In the remainder of this book, I'm going to show you how to experience exactly the same thing.

All my life, I had seen and experienced myself, according to my spells, as a miserable, frustrated, sad, loser—certain that I didn't deserve the best. My life had been that train wreck of disasters, failed relationships and loss.

After the breakthrough, everything I had strained and struggled and wrestled to try to change shifted effortlessly by itself. Money took care of itself, and I became totally happy, with amazing relationships, literally living the dream. And in frickin' Hawaii!!!

In Summary

After investing in every type of program about business, money, self-help, personal development, Law of Attraction, etc., and after generating $161 million in business; I ended up homeless and suicidal.

Then in a matter of minutes I had a breakthrough that completely turned everything around!

From a living hell to the paradise of my dreams.

This Core Paradigm Shift changed everything for me.

And, most miraculous of all, the breakthrough I experienced revealed to me the most wondrous thing to me:

My "gift" was not a curse. I came into this world to be a catalyst for change for millions of people. ALL of the hell I went through, the miserable childhood, the abuse, all of the broken relationships, all of the business disasters, all of the people whom I loved who left, ALL of it was actually the Universal Self (the Highest Me) preparing and grooming me for my mission!

A few months after the shift, I received the guidance to end my involvement with the business I was working with. I was guided to the mind-blowing vision of: Using my gift to help 300,000,000 people to experience their own Core Paradigm Shift, to dissolve the illusion of problems, to access their infinite self—Infinite Intelligence—and ever-present guidance so that they can Consciously Create the Body, Health, Business, Wealth, Relationships, Life and World of their dreams.

I spend my days and nights helping people all around the world to experience their own "homeless to Hawaii" miracle. Now, of course you probably aren't homeless, and Hawaii might not be your dream. I'm here to help you get from where you are to where you want to be—whatever that means for you.

In the last five years, largely on my own, with no idea of how to create or run such a "business," the Universe has helped me to touch tens of thousands of people around the world, and inspire them to take their first step into Total Personal Freedom.

Over the past few months, I have watched in awe as the Universe has brought and assembled an A-Team of brilliant, love-inspired geniuses around me, and with the launch of this book, we are about to begin to multiply those "thousands served" into the millions very rapidly.

Secrets of a Conscious Creator: On Skepticism
"Brian, I still have a lot of skepticism, and I just don't believe in the Law of Attraction or Spells or miracles or anything like that. Do you have any words for me?"

Answer: Okay, you're going to be blocked and unable to move forward unless and until we clear that. Right now, we are at a fork in the road.

On one side, you are skeptical and want to remain so. In that case, it is best to put this book down and get back to your life. In a few days, weeks or maybe years, the unhealed wounds and un-dealt-with issues will almost definitely have kicked your ass adequately to turn that skepticism into curiosity. The book will be here waiting for you.

On the other side, you simply feel skeptical and want to resolve it.

So I'm going to invite you to—and help you to—suspend your disbelief.

Take a few deep breaths. Relax. Recall a time when you experienced deja vu, or some sense of knowing something you "should not have been able to know." Maybe it was a premonition. We have all had those magical moments.

Now, as you consider this, be completely honest and ask a question you probably have never asked before, "Is that something that rarely happens, or might it be something that is always there…but that *I've rarely been open enough to sense?*"

Once you accept the possibility of the second option, and allow yourself to sense and know the obvious truth, things will begin to shift for you.

If you are able to tap in and tune into those energies EVER, even ONCE, then you could be tapping into them more frequently—maybe all of the time!

And if that is true, then what will happen when you find the switch—the key to the door or the gateway that enables you to be ONE with that info?"

Check in for a moment. Can you really deny that, on some level, you know in your bones that the Universe is all One Eternal Energy? And that you are IT?

**Have a question for me? See what others
have asked and ask your own question at
www.BreakYourSelfHelpAddiction.com/ama.
I want to hear from you.**

If you are really feeling skeptical about this information, but really WANT to trust and give your doubtful mind some support so it can join you in this journey, here is a powerful "extra-credit" exercise:

90-Day Skepticism-Elimination Experiment

Here's a quick experiment for the next 90 days, which is the period of time generally required for a total life transformation. (Not just for creating a new habit, but changing everything.)

For the next 90 days, here is what I want you to do.

Wake up in the morning and if there is some drink you absolutely hate, grab a cup of that drink. The purpose here is to become miserable. Then sit in the darkest corner you can find. Put your head in your hand in the posture of deep depression.

As you drink that nasty drink that you don't like, I want you to visualize for 15 minutes every morning for 90 days the most horrific disaster and disease possible coming into your life and making your life a living hell. Just envision that for 15 minutes. Every day. For 90 days.

Are you ready to start this experiment?

I hear you saying, "Brian there is no way I would do that," to which I say, "Why not?"

The truth is that both you and I know full well that if you focus on something with that level of intensity, it, or something like it, is going to come about.

So let's suspend our doubts as we move on.

Oh, and please choose to "pass" on my experiment!

Two Questions

So, now you know my story. That I was in hell and one Core Paradigm Shift changed everything in seconds. And you know my promise with this book is to help you to have the same experience.

Here are two questions to help you more fully open yourself to the information that I am about to share with you. Please breathe deeply, and take a moment to really feel each question, and the energies that arise in your body in response.

Question #1

"How would I feel if I were totally free in every area of life? How would I feel being able to go where I want, when I want, with whom I want, free to buy, sell, give, share, and donate the way I really want?"

Question #2

"How would I feel if I had infinite power, limitless guidance, and the emotional presence to navigate every life situation with ease and grace?"

Take a moment to really FEEL the energies in your body responding to those two questions. Suspend your doubts and let's...

Chapter 2

Make the
Unconscious Conscious

"The secret is to make the implicit explicit."
—Krishnamurti

One of the biggest secrets to life that I've learned is the necessity of making the unconscious conscious—the implicit into the explicit.

You are, right now, in this moment, already perfectly masterfully creating your life.

You don't need any courses on manifestation. You are always perfectly, flawlessly manifesting your life.

The issue is that you've been doing it largely unconsciously. You've been unknowingly, unconsciously creating and literally forming your life out of the plethora of implicit beliefs, assumptions, rules, values and paradigms (Spells) that you are semi-consciously or unconsciously living.

My mission with my Conscious Creators' work and my mission with this book is to give you the tools to be able to go from unconsciously creating hell to consciously creating your own heaven on earth, and expanding that out through your family and through your work, and through your whole world.

Your True Identity

Please try on a concept with me for a minute. Close your eyes and take a few deep breaths. Imagine that:

- …what you are includes all of the knowledge, information, and wisdom that has ever been and will ever be…
- …what you truly are includes all of the power that creates all of the universe and universes…
- …what Napoleon Hill called Infinite Intelligence—is flowing, without limit, inexhaustibly, into you and through you 24/7,… and creating YOUR universe through YOU.

Imagine that this, not all of the conditioning you took on as a child, is your true identity.

In this book, and in the accompanying videos, I will show you how to focus your awareness in such a way that you intentionally aim and channel all of that knowledge, information, wisdom, and power into the *intentional conscious creation* of everything that you want—to make the body, health, business, wealth, relationships, life and world of your dreams.

As we go deeper, I will also show you how to dissolve, dismantle, and demolish all of the things that you have thus far created and manifested, as you unintentionally, unknowingly lived out of all of your implicit (programmed) assumptions, beliefs, rules, values, and old paradigms (spells).

Other Concepts Coming Up

We're also going to look at some other key concepts that will help your mind believe and understand, so that it can willingly join and support you as you begin to live what you know is true. We're going to help your mind through that process. (This is a very crucial missing key in much of the more "spiritually-advanced" personal development work available. If you've ever encountered a powerful, "obvious" spiritual truth and then felt unable to really be able to integrate it into your life, this missing element was probably partially at play.)

A lot of self-help approaches only work with the mind, and a lot of spiritual approaches try to go in direct opposition to the mind, but neither of those ways is sustainable, and neither really works.

Another big myth out there is that meditation and "mind quieting" can do what's needed to make your ideal life happen. Perhaps they can help, to a certain extent, but the odds are high that you have felt bad about yourself for not being able to meditate or quiet your mind enough. Or maybe you have been able to meditate for years, but you're not seeing any changes in the deepest pain-spots of your life. We're going to dissolve all of that.

We're also going to look at the concept of "spells." I've referred to this concept already, but what is a spell? Isn't that just like a fairy tale idea? You're going to find that spells are actually very real.

You'll be surprised to learn that you have put yourself under hundreds, if not thousands, of them. As a child, you allowed society, education, the medical system, governmental systems, religious systems to place you under tens of thousands of spells. You're going to understand what they are, and how they work. You're also going to get access to tools to dissolve them.

We're also going to look at the "Theory of Constraints", which is one of the most radically powerful business concepts ever formulated. It is outrageously complex, but can be distilled into a simple idea that you can apply to any part of your life to experience quantum leaps in consciousness, ability, and freedom *in a matter of seconds.*

We're also going to talk about paradigms and the levels of transformation that are available to you. We'll take a closer look at how you got to where you are and how you can move out of it. We're going to look at how shifting your core paradigm to the "Level Five Paradigm" is the necessary beginning.

This "core paradigm shift" is *the* key missing ingredient in almost all approaches to personal development and self-help.

Secrets of a Conscious Creator: On the "Fear of Success"
"Brian, I am afraid that I might have a fear of success? Is there such a thing, or is it all just fear of failure?"

Answer: I say, "It's only fear. It's all the same fear." We're going to talk deeply about emotions, what they are and why they matter.

We're going to talk about how to become a conscious master of your emotions, directing your emotions to actually serve you, as well as following your emotions into more and more of the miracles you truly want to live in.

For now, I just want to acknowledge the reality that fear often comes up when a person begins to actually take step into a life of miracles—or even a life that "works".

You've probably heard about the amygdala, which is a part of the brain that some refer to as the "lizard brain" or the ancient, ancestral brain that is there to keep you safe. (We'll talk about this much more deeply later.)

Your mind—particularly this old part of your mind—is not designed to be the driver of your life.

The mind is designed to be the navigator, but through our programming, through our training as children in our modern cultures, we've been taught to actually "let go of the wheel" on many topics. And when you release the wheel, the mind automatically grabs it and begins to drive.

We've abdicated the throne and given the keys to the mind.

But when the mind is driving, it really only understands one job, and that is to keep you safe. The only way that it knows to do that is to keep everything exactly the way that it is. In effect, it jerks the wheel to "lock" a hard left and keeps it there. (This is why you may eventually begin to notice that you are going in circles—that the landscape is beginning to be strangely familiar…)

When we get ready to make a change, we immediately come face to face with all of the things that we ever placed between ourselves and that change, which includes all of our fears.

So this is normal. But normal is rarely beneficial. So…

Let's do something now to help make this change you're going through easier and smoother.

EXERCISE

Please write down a short paragraph in answer to this question: "What do I fear might happen if I were to dare believe and actually step towards the life I want—to dare to take action towards it?"

Take a few minutes with this question and then answer as honestly as you possibly can. To jog your thoughts (although your own answer will be the most helpful to you), here's an example:

"I'm afraid I might fail. It might not work and I might find out that this system is another one that is all BS. I'm afraid I'll lose my friends / family. I'm afraid I will evolve but then my partner won't, and I'll end up losing them or having to leave them or, worse, having to stay with them and pretend." etc.

As we go through this book, I'll show you exactly how to dissolve your fears and obstacles, including the ones you just wrote down, so that you can be in a state of ever-present power and certainty where, moment by moment, you're creating more and more of the life you really want.

One of my clients, Karen, was suffering from severe fear of "putting herself out there". She's a brilliant coach with a lot to offer. She had wanted to start putting her info into YouTube videos to share with her audience but was paralyzed by fear. A few days ago, I was doing a Livestream video and I offered to do a few public Spellbreaks. Karen found the courage to show up and to come on video with me for a Spellbreak. She emailed me earlier today that the knot in her stomach that had been there for 30 years is GONE. It dissolved during our short session—and days later, it is still gone.

Have a question for me? See what others have asked and ask your own question at www.BreakYourSelfHelpAddiction.com/ama. I want to hear from you.

Chapter 3

Spells

"*We only see what we want to see; we only hear what we want to hear. Our belief system is just like a mirror that only shows us what we believe.*"

—Don Miguel Ruiz

I've mentioned "spells" a few times already, and it is time to fully address the idea.

I offer the radical proposition that, behind it all, "spells" are the ONLY cause of pain, frustration, sadness, procrastination, fear, difficulty, feeling overwhelmed, depression, body issues, negative emotions, and all business, money and success limitations.

There.

I said it.

I know, I know.

It sounds crazy.

So now let me give you the evidence. You decide.

The Reality of Spells

Throughout history, select people have held the knowledge of the reality of spells. In recent times, science and religion have largely altered or erased knowledge of them. For the majority of us, our only exposure to them today is through the "humorously superficial" form of cartoons or animated movies.

The gravity and reality of spells has been relegated to silliness and/or superstition.

In truth, spells are neither magical nor make-believe. And once you understand their inherent cost, they are definitely not silly.

A spell is a **mental, emotional, and/or psychological state** where one's behavior is quite literally dictated to them, on one or more topics or areas of life by unconscious drivers. When activated, the person **appears to have no ability to overcome his or her reactions to certain triggers.**

Think, "Snow White". When the trigger flipped, she went to sleep—and she was frozen in that state, unable to move, until she was set free by a kiss of love.

You might be surprised to find how "true" that scenario is. For you. For everybody else. And on soooooooooo many topics...

If heights don't bother you, then think about someone you know who is absolutely terrified of heights. He or she is under a spell that says, "heights are terrifying". It creates limiting behaviors and irrational reactions, and she is unable to see the roots of it.

Or someone who is terrified of dogs. She is trapped in the "dogs are terrifying" spell. It creates limiting behaviors and irrational actions that she can neither see nor alter.

Or think about someone who, no matter what she does, just can't make money. She has all the skills and knowledge, talent and awareness, the information like everyone else, but she just can't seem to make any money. She is under some form of, "money is hard" spell. Again, limiting behaviors and irrational actions follow. And she is unable to see or alter them.

The list is nearly endless.

GO DEEPER

Watch a powerful spell get dissolved right before your eyes. Check it out at www.BreakYourSelfHelpAddiction.com/ spellbreak-money

Is there an area of your life where you feel stuck?

Is there an area in which you seem to get irrationally afraid, angry, upset, or ineffective?

Have you tried to change some aspect of your life again and again, but it just doesn't change?

As I'll illustrate in just a moment, these painful areas of life are the result of a litany of spells.

The Endless Loop of Spells

We have all these spells on specific topics. They are closely related to beliefs. They run as "topic-sensitive" programs in our operating system.

They cluster into groups of spells called "rules" and "values". These run as full-scale programs in our systems.

Those clusters group at a higher level into paradigms. They make up "everything I know" on a specific topic—and they create your "worldview" on that topic.

All of the spells, beliefs, rules/values and paradigms related to "What I Am" make up your *Identity*. They guide your behaviors about relating to others and the world.

And, above it all, all of your beliefs, rules/values, paradigms and your Identity cluster into your SuperSpell—which is your Core Paradigm. Your Core Paradigm is the sum total of "everything I think and believe that I know".

And it prevents you from EVER being able to see, access, experience and alter "What Is".

It is shocking to realize that the vast majority of what we think and believe and "know" is utter, complete bulls***. All of it is purely the result of spells that we "bought" along the way, and which now dictate our lives, our circumstances and even our available responses to those circumstances.

What is the result? What is the outcome of all of the spells in our lives?

- We endlessly experience the same pains and frustrations
- We automatically judge people and things and alienate those closest to us
- We find ourselves in "the same relationship" again and again—even with "new" partners
- We begin to feel confused and wonder if we might secretly be crazy—at least on "x topic"
- We begin to feel hopeless and powerless—not knowing how we "got *that* again"
- We blame anything and anyone (Because we can't find the "hidden" cause, we feel certain that it must be something outside of ourselves)
- We decide we must have "lessons" to learn—and from this 'focus", we create an endless string of more and more lessons—never knowing how to make it stop
- The "lessons" Spell keeps us frozen in the belief that there "must be" a "Lesson Giver" up in the sky wanting to zap us every time we screw up

We find ourselves trying approach after approach to change things but find the boomerang coming back again and again.

We can't figure out why this keeps happening over and over and over, and this is where we get that feeling of being totally stuck.

As an important side-note, it is no secret that getting and having enough money is widely seen as the biggest challenge for most people in the world. Reading what you have read so far might lead you to believe that "money spells" are the issue.

Surprisingly, they almost never are.

Through working with thousands of people ranging from billionaires to the homeless, I have found that there is actually no such thing as a "money issue". It nearly all roots down in "lovability-and-deservability"-related spells.

That's why you can take every course on money, business, and success known to man. But if you have a huge magnet inside of you that says, "I can't have", "I don't deserve", or "If I get, I suffer", you will stay stuck until you break that "spell"—and change that paradigm.

The good news here: When you break your "spell," everything changes instantly around that "spell."

The better news: You can break your spells!

How I Became "The Spellbreaker"

After my miracle moment, I started to notice that, everywhere I went, people were showing up who wanted my help. Somehow, they knew that they could tell me their problems. Even more amazingly, they seemed to automatically know that I could help them.

Literally every day, one or more people showed up with their own issues, their own spells, on display, asking for my help. And, each and every time, the same Infinite Intelligence that facilitated my "miracle moment" showed up and showed me exactly how to help those people to dissolve their spells and step into freedom.

The work I did with those "early" clients has become the core of my Conscious Creators work, seminars, "Transformation to Liberation" retreats in Hawaii, events, programs and 1-on-1 work I do today.

I've spent the past 5 years fine-tuning and perfecting this work. And you'll be glad to know that, at the core of the Conscious Creators work is something I call "Spellbreaks". You'll learn more about those—including how to do a Self-Spellbreak—in the coming chapters.

GO DEEPER

Have you observed a repeating unpleasant pattern in your life? If it seems overwhelming, and if you're ready to transcend it, I'm happy to help. Keep reading the next chapters or learn more at www. BreakYourSelfHelpAddiction.com/Spellbreaks.

Secrets of a Conscious Creator: On Breaking Spells
How can I identify and get rid of my spells?

Answer: In this book, I'm going to a give you a powerful set of tools: the Basic Self-Spellbreak technique, as well as a complete Self-Spellbreak process.

As far as *identifying* your spells, the good news is that you never actually have to do this.

I personally invested between $30,000—$40,000 on multiple belief elimination programs and systems, and I gradually came to realize that it was largely a waste of time, energy and money. Not to say that belief elimination (finding your beliefs and eliminating them), doesn't work; it can.

But the "weird" reality is that we have potentially millions, or even billions of beliefs running through our bodies. To find them all and eliminate them would take forever—or probably about the same 13-15 billion years we took to create them all. ;-)

More to the point, though, it's very rare that any belief related to a topic is what is actually causing our results in that area of life.

Usually we have hidden beliefs about other disjointedly-connected things regarding our deservability, our lovability, the nature of the opposite sex, etc. that cause these problems, so I don't waste any time identifying the spells and I don't advise it.

Secrets of a Conscious Creator: On Spellbreaks
Will one Spellbreak solve all my problems, forever?

Answer: Breaking even one spell can create massive, wide-ranging, long-lasting results in one or more areas of life. A challenging reality, though, often arises after a powerful Spellbreak:

When one spell is broken, especially if it is a central spell (spanning multiple life areas), the next related spells rapidly arise to be met and dissolved.

If you understand and accept that we're all eternal co-creators of our shared universe, then you will find it enlightening to consider this: For the last fifteen billion years, since we created this universe, we've been testing these spells on ourselves and creating societal structures and people to cast spells upon us.

(If this concept is too far "out there" for you, that is perfectly OK. You can get massive results from Spellbreak work without accepting this idea.)

Again, we have layers and layers of spells, hierarchies of spells. These spells create beliefs. The beliefs constellate into higher levels of spells, which we call "rules" and "values". All of the spells, beliefs, rules and values about "what I am" becomes my Self-Image Spell or "Identity". And, finally, ALL of my beliefs, spells, rules, values and identity makes up my Core Paradigm Spell. (This will become very important in the next few chapters.)

When I do a Spellbreak Session with a client, they invariably experience a radical, instant, deep and lasting shift into freedom, ease and grace in one or more areas.

The larger the shift, the more freedom, ease and grace... and the more related spells show up to be dealt with. This often leads to me working with them more intensively to dissolve all of the spells relating to an area of life—or, sometimes, doing an intense-multi-day Liberation Session. At the end of the book, I'll share more of the options available to you if you want to go further.

**Have a question for me? See what others
have asked and ask your own question at
www.BreakYourSelfHelpAddiction.com/ama.
I want to hear from you.**

What We've Covered So Far

I've shared with you my story and a summary of several crucial, core concepts:

1. The fact that we are all creating our life, largely unconsciously
2. There is more available to us than we have been aware of
3. We want to move from unconsciously creating by default to consciously creating our lives
4. Spells are a reality
5. They are the real cause of *all problems*
6. They can be dissolved or "broken"
7. When they are broken, we can go from a lifetime of "homeless" to our "Hawaii" virtually overnight

Armed with this foundation, I'm going to reveal a "set of keys" that has the ability to begin to set you free—today. Literally in the next few minutes.

That is no exaggeration.

Here are…

5 Keys to Total Personal and Financial Freedom

- **Key One: Shift your CORE paradigm.**
- **Key Two: Become Present and Centered In Your Power**
- **Key Three: Focus On What You Want to Experience**
- **Key Four: Clear the past and Recapture Your Power**
- **Key Five: Become the Master**

Let's begin with Key One…

Chapter 4

The First Key: Shift Your Core Paradigm

"If you want to make small changes in your life, then work on your behaviors. If you want to make quantum-leap changes, work on your paradigms."
—**Dr. Stephen Covey**, *The 7 Habits of Highly Effective People*

What Creates the "Illusion of Problems"

Everyone has things in life that they really, really want that they seem unable to get.

Things that, no matter what they do, seem to stay just out of reach.

You have one or more of these, or you would not be reading this book. So, let's reflect for a moment. What is one of yours? Maybe it's the relationship of your dreams, the extra zero (or couple of zeros) at the right end of your bank account balance, or perhaps the ultimate dream home…

Similarly, everyone has things in life that they really, really don't want.

Things that, no matter what they do, seem to keep coming back.

That spouse or partner who keeps coming back with a different face, the living situation that always shows up again a few months after you relocate…

What if I told you that ALL of these things were caused by ONE thing?

One hidden cause? One invisible "core constraint".

One of the promises of this book is that I will help you dissolve the "Illusion of Problems."

What could I possibly mean by that?

Well, what if there was ONE issue, one hidden core constraint that was causing ALL of your problems? (Or, more accurately, causing the "illusion" of your problems.)

What if that ONE hidden core constraint was *the reason* why some of the things that you really, really want stay out of reach no matter what you do?

What if that ONE hidden core constraint was also the cause of ALL of the things that you really, really DON'T want, that keep showing up?

Incredibly, it really is true.

Hidden Core WHAT?

I'll show you how it is true in a very unusual way:

I'm going to introduce you to a powerful, practical, foundational business concept known as the **Theory of Constraints**.

Many years ago, as I was studying some of the greatest business minds of recent times, I stumbled across this idea, which many leaders hail as one of the most powerful business concepts ever discovered.

The TOC is incredibly complicated and there are thousands of pages of information you can study and investigate.

For our purposes, I've distilled it down into a really simple, very powerful example that will illustrate my point:

Imagine you wanted to win a footrace.

You did everything possible to prepare to do so.

You trained with the best trainer in the world for the last 5 years.

You shaved every hair off of your body to eliminate wind-drag.

You bought the best toe socks and put them on carefully—with no wrinkles.

You bought the best tailored shoes, and you put them on perfectly over your socks.

You are wearing blazing red skintight Speedos (you even *look* fast!).

You ate a perfect breakfast.

The wind is at your back, and you've spent the last 3 hours meditating and visualizing yourself crossing the finish line first.

You've literally done everything you can possibly do to condition and prepare yourself to win.

Question: What are your chances?

There's only one problem:

You have a truck parked on your foot!

One tiny detail. And now, the question again:

What are your chances?

Sheesh! Even the snail beside your other foot is going to kick your ass in this race.

The theory of constraints shows that you can do all the best possible preparations, and you can fine-tune every possible practice, but if you have a *major bottleneck* at some point, if you have a *significant constraint* in place, nothing can positively impact your results as much as the removal of the constraint.

Another key idea of the TOC is that you can waste a lot of time, money and energy doing *more* preparations, and taking *more* courses, and *more* programs, and *more* running practice, and *more* drilling "victory" into your mind, (or, perhaps *more* self-help programs) etc… But until you move the truck off your foot, you're really just wasting your time.

Do not gloss over this, please, for your own sake. If you reflect on it for a moment, it leads to a *massively powerful, freeing and very exciting truth*.

If you have been "stuck", no matter how long you have been stuck, you can simply find and remove your Primary Core Constraint and you'll be able to move. Now. Today.

But it gets even better! When you finally move the truck off your foot (remove your constraint), all of a sudden—all of the time, the energy and money that you've invested in training, preparing, and visualizing (and into the self-help addiction), all of a sudden, all of that comes to life and is multiplied in value.

This is true of any constraint you might identify and remove.

However, when you shift your *Core Constraint,* everything can change at once. Specifically, when you shift your Core Paradigm, ALL of the personal development, energy work, self-help programs and goal-setting work—all of it is activated and brought into power in that moment.

One of my clients, Jack, was pretty skeptical about how one thing could change everything. Today, he's one of my biggest fans. His words, "It's amazing—everything changes… I mean, my business, business bank account, my relationships, everything. It really is amazing."

So, what does this TOC (Theory of Constraints) stuff have to do with spells, becoming a Conscious Creator and personal/financial freedom?

I'm so grateful you asked, because that is where we are going next.

We've Been All Wrong

It is time for a big shift away from what we "knew" to be true.

Big changes usually emerge into our world from big thinkers and seers. And the rest of us usually take our sweet time getting with the program...

A few decades ago there was this really smart guy named Einstein. When asked to explain the universe, Einstein said:

"Concerning the universe and matter, we've been all wrong. What we've called matter is actually light energy whose vibration has been lowered so as to make it perceptible to the senses. There is no matter."

Many people considered Einstein to be the smartest man of his time. He thought otherwise.

When a reporter asked Einstein, "How does it feel to be the smartest man alive?" He replied, "I don't know. You'd have to ask the smartest man alive. That's Nikola Tesla."

If you check in with Mr. Tesla, he said the exact same thing:

"If you want to understand the secrets of the universe, you have to think in terms of energy, frequency and vibration."

Now, you may be beginning to see a pattern here. Let's go even deeper.

In the number one best-selling personal development/business book of all time, Napoleon Hill said:

"Whatever the mind of man can conceive and believe, it can achieve... Behind what we call matter ... It's all infinite intelligence."

Einstein: "There is no matter."
Tesla: "It's all vibration."
Hill: "It's all Infinite Intelligence."

So, these three geniuses of recent times, as well as all of the spiritual masters and seers throughout all time, have all said it: There is actually no physical universe here—*at all.*

It's just light energy—vibrating (blinking on and off—in and out of existence) at specific frequencies.

Today, finally, the quantum physicists are proving beyond the shadow of a doubt that what we've been calling a Physical Universe is a non-physical energy vibrating in and out of existence.

We perceive it as being physical—and we become locked into what Deepak Chopra calls, "the superstition of materialism".

We are literally trapped by our own Core Paradigm of physicality!

In the next few pages, I'm going to go much deeper into that and show you the actual mechanisms on how that works. You'll get a great insight into manifestation and how to directly, consciously—on purpose—create and manifest everything you want to experience. (And how to stop manifesting what you don't.)

What if you had a belief, a core belief, that was holding you back and you didn't know what it was? What if that belief, paradigm or spell made you unable to see "truth" by pretending to be the "truth"?

You would experience a set of incomprehensible life experiences.

You would find things that you have pushed away—continually coming back.

You would find things that you desire—continually eluding you.

You would seem to be powerless to change them.

You would frequently catch yourself "doing it again", acting in a way that makes no sense to yourself or to others.

You would make a resolution on New Year's Day—and then find yourself making it again 365 days later.

You would feel like a victim of circumstance or of "fate".

You literally would not be able to see or understand what was holding you back because you were living in that paradigm!

You would be as oblivious to the hidden core paradigm as a fish is oblivious to water.

Does this situation seem familiar to you? Maybe a little bit?

The minute that you accept the possibility that there might be one core hidden constraint—one constraint that's actually causing everything you don't want to show up and causing everything you do want to stay away—you've got to ask *the question.*

The question is, "What is *my* hidden Core Constraint?"

I'm proposing that almost everyone on the planet has the same Core Constraint.

And it is a weird one.

Incredibly, it is that you believe that there is a **physical** universe and that you're a **physical** part of it—separate from it—*and that you have to deal with it **physically**.*

It's you against the world in every aspect and area of life. You're "living" your body, your health, your business, your relationship with money and wealth, your relationships with other people and your relationship with life and the world—you're actually living all of it in direct opposition to the fundamental truth of the universe and yourself.

And—you're doing it in **the most difficult, stressful way possible**!!!

You have been living as if Newtonian physics were true, and we've known now for decades that it's not. Newton basically said we're living as separate little chunks of meat in a giant clock machine that's driven by fate and we're all basically screwed. (Don't believe me? Look up "clockwork universe.")

Living our lives according to that lie is exhausting, it's miserable, it's destructive to your body, it's the cause of all problems.

It's an illusion and it's unnecessary.

Fortunately, there is a way out.

The Power of a CORE Paradigm Shift

When I talk to people about what I do, I often run into initial skepticism. Many people just can't imagine how changing "one thing" can begin to create change in every area of life at once.

It can.

When you change your CORE (or central) paradigm, which is the SuperSpell that contains every issue that's holding you back, of course everything begins to shift to meet the awareness it brings.

Before we go of all the way into this, let's get a bit clearer on paradigms.

What Exactly Is a Paradigm and What Is *Your* Core Paradigm?

A paradigm is a way of seeing the world on a *specific* topic. It's a filter your mind uses for *that* topic. It dictates what you can see and think and experience on *that* topic. (More on that in a moment, when we begin to talk about the nervous system component known as the "RAS".)

A *topical paradigm* creates and dictates all of your thoughts, ideas, beliefs, experiences—all of your results on *that* topic.

Your *Core Paradigm* is the summary, the composite of ALL of your paradigms on *every* topic.

It dictates and creates everything you can see and think and experience on *every* topic.

It creates and dictates all of your results on every topic.

If that sounds far-fetched to you, just hang on and observe.

Remember our discussion on spells in the last chapter?

Each of us was born into a culture that is under the influence of a massive number of spells.

Our culture includes our parents, our religion, and our schools—each of which programmed us to embrace different spells; and of course, we believed them.

Our Core Paradigm is the combination of all of those spells, a massive "SuperSpell".

As I said, for reasons we are going to see in a moment, your Core Paradigm, or your SuperSpell, dictates everything you will ever experience—without exception. This ties to a point I made earlier and asked you to really take note of:

**There is no continuity other than what
we think and believe that we know.**

Those things you don't want that keep coming back are the fruits of your paradigms.

The things you do want that stay out of reach do so because of your paradigms.

So the bottom line is this:

If your life is not the way you want it to be (remember our Theory of Constraints), you can work on everything—your practices, your language, your behaviors, your potentials, and everything else—while experiencing little to no results, or temporary, short-lived results.

Because of this, *nothing* is more critically important than changing your paradigm—breaking that SuperSpell—releasing that Core Constraint.

Nothing will create the magnitude of results—and nothing will match the speed of results of addressing that over-arching SuperSpell.

The 4 "Lower" Paradigms

The first step towards changing your Core Paradigm is to get clear on your existing one! Let's do that now.

There are 4 pre-existing "lower" core paradigms on the planet. Let me walk you through them very briefly here. As we do this, be observant and see if anyone you know fits in them.

In my private and group work, I go much deeper into this information. My purpose with this section of the book is to give you the absolute minimum-required info on the pre-existing paradigms that will enable you to fully use and benefit from the rest of the book.

The First Paradigm—The Meatsuit

In the First Paradigm, one sees oneself as a "meat suit in a machine", separate from all the rest of existence and totally controlled by "external forces"— driven by fate.

People living in the Meatsuit Paradigm are basically cavemen and cavewomen, (and there are a surprising number of them still among us). They believe they have to go out and do battle with the world, in order to "bring home the bananas and be able to feed the family". It can be an exhausting existence, permeated with stress, disconnection and disease. These people often die young. They are doing their best to live—under a very difficult paradigm.

Possible traits of someone operating from the first paradigm:

- Very physically-focused
- Frequently aggressive—seemingly without reason
- Reactive, jumps to conclusions
- Victim mentality—it's everyone else's fault

The Second Paradigm—The Mind

In the Second Paradigm, one sees oneself as a bit "above" the dumb meatsuits, but still very much separate and having to deal with "external forces". They just do it "smarter".

The "mind folks" among us say, "I'm not a dumb ass meat suit. No, I'm way smarter than that. I hire meat suits and they go out and do stuff for me and I'm able to get way more bananas faster… more, better bananas and I live my life on a whole other level." However, it's really no different. It's still them against the world—battling, struggling and straining. And in the end, they know, fate will win. They, also, are doing their best, but their manipulations and controlling tendencies often alienate them from others.

Possible traits of someone operating from the second paradigm:

- Disconnected
- Pessimistic
- Manipulative and controlling
- Overly sarcastic, jaded

The Third Paradigm—"Religiosity"

In the Third Paradigm, one begins to trust that they might be connected to, or able to connect with, something bigger that can help them deal with the "external forces". They get trapped, though, in the structure, usually unconsciously.

The third level is when we begin to get into religion and religious beliefs. We begin to say, "Maybe there's more to all this."

Now, they still have to bring home the bananas, but they're doing it in a religious structure that gives them a larger set of beliefs and a larger perspective. Yet often, when it gets down to it, they are still stuck—and now it is with the added weight of trying to live by externally-created rules. Like everyone living in the first and seconds paradigms, these people are doing their best to live "by the rules". They often feel deeply frustrated and sad that "they must be getting it wrong".

Possible traits of someone operating from the third paradigm:

- Judgmental & Self-Righteous
- Inflexible and indignant
- Priding themselves on a morality that is not necessarily their own
- Hypocritical

The Fourth Paradigm—"Being Spiritual"

In the Fourth Paradigm, one claims connection with the Divine, yet still believes (almost always unconsciously) that the Divine is an "external force". They walk a tight-rope of "knowing" spiritual things in their mind, and "trying to live them", while wrestling with doubts and feeling confused about why it isn't really working for them.

The fourth paradigm is the paradigm of beginning to outgrow religion and being or becoming "spiritual". These folks are doing their best to move beyond religion. They are sincere. One of these people might think, "Wait a minute. Maybe there's really more to this. I'm not just a meat suit. I'm not just a mind. I don't need to just subscribe to someone else's pre-programmed religious truth…"

The "spiritual" people are doing their best, but *they are trying to reach their inner peace and prosperity, without having access to the true inner power that makes it possible.*

(As a side note: I work with a LOT of "spiritual" people. Yoga teachers, Law of Attraction teachers, coaches, mentors, energy-workers, therapists, psychologists, and "healers" who have reached the end of their rope. They know the truth, but they feel incredibly stuck, as they have not found the missing links you are about to discover in the next chapters.)

Possible traits of someone operating from the fourth paradigm:

- Surface-spiritual—talk the talk but isn't fully able to walk the walk
- Not fully grounded despite their best efforts and serious practice
- Usually has a very difficult time with money/abundance

No one lives in one paradigm their whole life, or in every part of their life. They might live in one paradigm in a particular area of their life for a time, until they clear or transcend a life-issue. Then, they can ascend to the next paradigm in that area—even while living in a different paradigm in all other areas.

Every person living in each of those four paradigms are imprisoned by a specific constraint.

Well, wait a minute... Aren't spiritual people operating from the absolute highest level? What could be above that?

Scarcity Paradigm vs. Abundance Paradigm (The Level 5 Paradigm)
Before I answer, let me give you a clue:

All 4 paradigms are actually a trap. Yes, even the "spiritual" paradigm.

All four are a trap of *scarcity*.

Did you notice that there was a common theme of "external forces" in all four of those "lower" paradigms? If there is anything external to us that has power, then we are potential victims.

And if there is anything external to us that has power *over us*, we are "screwed".

In truth, there are no external forces. None.

In a moment, when we discuss The Level 5 Paradigm, everything will become clear. Your paradigm will begin to shift even as you read the next section.

For now, let me leave this discussion with a hint.

When a person living in the "spiritual" paradigm talks about abundance, they generally mean "more". They are speaking of a Level 5 Paradigm concept from a 4th Paradigm awareness. They mean "more money for *one* or for *some*"—or "more of everything for *one* or for *some*".

But it is almost cliché that most "spiritual people" can't seem to get their life in order and they generally experience the opposite of the abundance they speak of.

When a person living in The Level 5 Paradigm speaks of abundance, they mean infinite—limitless. Not "more".

So this Core Paradigm shift to the Level Five Paradigm is actually where efforts at transformation <u>end</u> and liberation <u>begins</u>.

It's the elusive, missing piece that I'd experienced in virtually all of the extensive self-help and personal development work that I'd done prior to my Miracle Moment.

The absence of The Level 5 Paradigm Truth in so much of today's personal development work is why I, and so many others, ended every book, program and seminar with hope and determination, only to wake up 3 or 4 days later right smack dab where we began—just a bit more jaded than before.

That is over for you and me. We are going to begin to make that core shift now.

Are you ready?

Then, let's look at....

The Level 5 Paradigm—Oneness

Remember my poolside Miracle Moment?

I went from the *idea* that everything is energy to the actual experience of it. I went from the *idea* of infinite possibilities into the actual experience of it.

As you consider The Level 5 Paradigm, you will find yourself doing the same thing.

In The Level 5 Paradigm, you're not separate. You're not a meat suit. You're not a mind. You're not trying to live according to ANY religious rules. You're no longer even trying to "be spiritual".

And you're no longer subject to any "external forces".

In The Level 5 Paradigm, you realize that there is an energy, an eternal complete perfect energy that is flowing *from eternity into time and space.*

The Eternal Energy never "leaves" eternity because at the eternal level, nothing changes.

It's flowing into, or, more accurately, vibrating in-and-out-of time and space, creating this illusion of a universe. This is the energy that the quantum physicists are detecting popping in and out of existence, vibrating its specific frequencies—all of that energy is infinite and eternal.

It's beyond birth or death.

It's not created or destroyed.

It's beyond any ideas of good and bad.

It's beyond any ideas of right and wrong.

It's even beyond positive and negative.

All of those imprisoning ideas and everything else in the entire universe is informed and enlivened by this eternal energy projecting out of eternity into time and space and vibrating its specific frequencies.

If everything in the universe is that energy, then what are you?

You are that.

You're beyond birth and death.

You're beyond good and bad.

You're beyond right and wrong.

You're beyond positive and negative.

You're actually perfect, eternal and complete with no flaws, faults or badness—or goodness. You're beyond all ideas.

That's your truth.

However, we were born into a sleepwalking, spellbound society filled with infinite beings disguised as humans. We were programmed with the lie of Newtonian physics.

You were born into a world of parents, medical systems, educational systems, governmental systems, religious systems—and each of those systems had its lies/spells to perpetuate.

You got programmed with the lies and you got completely stuck in that set of beliefs, spells, rules, values and paradigms.

We are going to begin to move those spells out. But before we do, let's get clear on just exactly HOW we learned these "spells."

GO DEEPER

Note: This next section is pretty deep and intense. When I share it visually, I find that my audiences absorb it more completely and are able to better use the information.

If you prefer, you can go to this page and watch this short video to see it.

www.BreakYourSelfHelpAddiction.com/Physical

Better yet, watch the short video and then read it and fully integrate it before moving on.

HOW We Learned These "Spells"

In a moment, we are going to fully peel back the curtain on the quantum-physical, meta-physical and spiritual aspects of this. But, first, let's look at it from a purely physical position.

We were born surrounded by Gods and Goddesses. I mean, they had to be Gods and Goddesses, right?

We were unable to really speak or move around, lying there peeing and pooping in our diapers. We couldn't even get a drink or a meal without yelling and screaming for it. We needed those Gods and Goddesses for everything!

And these Gods and Goddesses were walking, talking, driving, moving, sitting, dancing, eating and drinking unassisted. Looking up at those amazing beings, we were amazed; and we saw and heard them sharing their words, their ideas, their emotions with each other—and with us.

To everything they said, we said to ourselves, "The God or Goddess is speaking. So, what they say MUST be true." Then they said more, and we said, "I'll buy that."

We were put under the "spell" of whatever they were talking about. We developed unconscious beliefs about each topic.

Deeper still, as babies, we had not yet been programmed with the lie that we only have 5 senses. We were still completely telepathic and able to sense and read emotions.

So, on top of hearing their words and sounds, we felt their feelings. And we bought those, too. *We decided those feelings were about us—or that they were actually ours.*

When we did something they didn't like, they told us that we were "bad". We said, "I'll buy that."

The "I'm a bad boy or bad girl" spell was switched on. All of a sudden, blockages, doubt and uncertainty became a part of our operating system.

They told us we were separate from everything else and we said, "I'll buy that." We fell under the "spell of separation." The unconscious beliefs locked into place and now fear, pain, hopelessness, and loneliness became part of our operating system.

They told us about "death". When someone in the family/inner circle exited their bodies, we learned that everything they said about "death" was true. We bought it, including the emotions they felt and expressed. The unconscious beliefs locked into place and now the "spell of 'people die and it is sad'" was cast. Sadness and misery around the natural and inevitable "exiting of bodies" became a part of our operating system.

They told us the rules about money, business and success. Forget about the fact that it was all bulls***. Trust me: What Warren Buffett's family taught him regarding "the rules of money, business and success" and what you and I were taught by our family about "the rules of money, business and success" are not the same. So it was not truth, it was just rules, just spells; and we said, "I'll buy that."

Then we got the "success/money is hard", spell. We embraced the unconscious beliefs which now create difficulty, complication, stress, *resistance to wealth* and procrastination in our operating system.

Along the way, they told us what we are. And this was most confusing of all, because different people told us different things about ourselves.

I don't know what they told you but I know what I took to be the core of the message they told me: "You are a stupid, ugly, worthless piece of s***." Just like we all always do, I said "I'll buy that."

Then we took on the "self-image spell." And embraced the unconscious beliefs and feelings of self-hate, hopelessness, confusion, frustration, procrastination, and fear. All of these things then became part of our operating system.

So all these things we were taught to believe; those crazy ideas like "I'm bad," "I'm not enough," "I don't deserve it," "I'm not safe," "God is angry with me," "money is evil," etc. All these limits became part of our "self-image spell."

Do you begin to see the radical truth now? Can you see why I invested so many pages setting this up?

Well, we are about to go even deeper.

This next point is one of the most crucial points in the entire book. The extent to which you "get" this, will be a key determining factor in how much you will be able to take away in the form of breakthroughs, insights, freedom and awesomeness.

Please take a few deep breaths and really relax and then read the next sentence.

It is impossible for a human being to consistently behave in a manner that is inconsistent with her own "self-image spell."

Now read that a couple of times. It is really *that* important.

In other words, since very early childhood, you have not been acting, creating or living from your true infinite identity.

Who you *are* is an infinite, unlimited, perfect, eternal, complete, amazing, "Being of Light," projecting from eternity into time and space, brother or sister of mine.

However, you have been unconsciously acting and creating your life from what you have unconsciously agreed that you are—from the summary of your spells.

So in one or more areas of life, you have been constantly in opposition to your true self.

With your mind and will-power, (the very least of your resources) you've been struggling, fighting and resisting the Infinite and Eternal part of you that is carrying out your deepest programming.

In other words, an incredibly giant, massive, infinite part of yourself is reaching out and carrying out the commands of all your "spells"—bad boy, bad girl, don't deserve, can't have, not worthy.

And this tiny little fraction of a particle of yourself, your conscious mind, is trying to overcome *that*!

And it is going to continue, until, like Sleeping Beauty, the kiss awakens you from your dream. (Almost makes you want to pucker up now, doesn't it?)

Now that I've framed the concept of where we come from within a *physical* perspective, let's go beyond the nuts and bolts and into the quantum physics perspective, combined with the *spiritual/energetic* point of view.

It's going to get weird. And it's the key to driving home the deepest truths of The Level 5 Paradigm, the universe, and you.

GO DEEPER

Note: As with the last section, this next section is pretty deep and intense.

You will get the most benefit from this section if you watch the video and then read the section below.

www.BreakYourSelfHelpAddiction.com/Spiritual

The Creation Myth (Or More Accurately, Subatomic Magic)

Now that we have established the critical importance of your Core Paradigm and have considered it from the "physical" position, let's look it at through the eyes of Science and Spirituality. (Science, so your mind can see and trust the truth of it; and Spirit, so I can express to you that which can't be conveyed with words.)

Throughout this section, I'm going to continually blend these two elements, Science and Spirit—into that all-important KEY to understanding the incomprehensible: The Creation Myth.

Every religion and spiritual tradition that deals with "The Beginning" does so through a story, a myth. And to be clear from the start, a myth is not a lie. Exploring unspeakable truth through a myth is a miracle formed by the fusion of story, allegory, symbolism and even poetry, to convey the transcendent truth—which is truly beyond words.

This Creation Myth I'm about to share is not "THE Truth" any more than ANY creation myth is "THE Truth." It is "**A** truth", and it is "my truth", based on everything I've ever learned, studied and experienced.

So please know that I am not asking you to believe it.

I am encouraging you to try it on and to reflect on it.

This information has helped thousands of people around the world to take their first step into true freedom. I trust it will do the same for you. Take a few deep breaths. Suspend your doubts for a moment, and be open to what's being shared.

In The Beginning...

In the beginning there was—and there *is*—nothing. No thing. No things. No time. No space.

Note that I said "was" *and* "is."

This is because "the beginning" happens to bring Eternity (outside of and BEYOND all time) into Time.

(Take a moment to re-read that sentence if necessary.)

The Eternal Reality has never changed and can never change.

It IS. Now.

This Nothing which emerges from Eternity is a very special and magical kind of Nothing—because this Nothing is "secretly" the infinite limitless capacity to be and to become Anything and Everything. An Eternal Being of Limitless, Expanding Energy.

This Infinite Eternal Being dwells in Bliss Throughout Eternity.

Dwelling in eternal bliss for all eternity ... bliss, bliss, bliss... omm, omm, omm ... eternal bliss forever... and it gets kinda, well, boring.

This Infinite Being has *nowhere to go* because, at the eternal level, *there is no space.*

It has *nothing to do* because, at the eternal level, *there is no "thing" or "things."*

It can't *experience* anything because, at the eternal level, *there is no time.* No change is possible. Therefore, no *experience* is possible.

Now, this is a critical, crucial point, so please take a few deep breaths and become centered. Then, read the next point.

Ready? OK, read and feel this:

"Experience" requires Limitation.

Did you get that? It's a critical point, and the more deeply and fully you "get" it, the more it will guide you into living in Heaven on Earth.

At the eternal level, there is no possibility of location, movement, or change—no possibility of experience. Infinite (limitless) Being has to introduce limitation in order to have experience.

Creation and Light

Back to our story…

Our Infinite Eternal Limitless Being said, "You know what? I REALLY want to have some experience… I think I am going to create something because I want to do something. There's nothing to do. I can't have any experience here, 'blissing' in eternity with nowhere to go and nothing to do.

I want to have EXPERIENCE.

"So I'm going to make a universe. I'll create the illusion of time and space. Up and down. Hot and cold. Here and there. Night and day. Dark and light. Heaven and Hell. This is gonna be FUN!!!!!"

But then, the realization came… "Wait a minute, wait a minute. Damn, there's nothing here to make a universe out of."

The game was over before it began.

But then, being Infinitely Capable, our Superhero Infinite Being had another realization, "You know what? I can DO this. I will make a Universe out of the only thing that exists—which is myself."

So it said, "Let me just make a division so that it seems like there's something here. Let there be light; yes, that's it—LIGHT!" And now there was light and darkness.

So, about 13 billion to 15 billion years ago (depending on who you listen to) that light and darkness split. And it has split somewhere in the neighborhood of a billion trillion quadrillion quintillion times, ever-complicating itself into ever more complex subtleties ever since then.

Why? Amazingly, the answer is very simple:

It (You) did it, and it does it, to have *experience.*

Not to work out some kind of Karma—which is a concept which It (You) invented in order to have more rich experience.

Not to finally get to Heaven! Duh! Where do you think It is at all times?!?!

The Infinite, Eternal One—All That Is—has disguised itself as a Universe—and, more importantly to you and me, it has disguised itself as every seemingly separate "thing" in that Universe (including you) for the purpose of having experience.

All of the great seers and sages, knowers and teachers have been saying it all along:

"All is One." "There is Only That—and I Am That."

Of course, the masses weren't ready to hear that, so most of those teachers were boiled, baked, burned at the stake, crucified or thrown into volcanoes. (Ouch!!!)

In a moment, we'll look at how the "truth" that has been hidden for sooo long was picked up by science over the last several decades, but first, we have to consider one more radically empowering truth that arises from our "Creation Myth".

There is a joke about "redneck bars" that refers to "leaving your gun at the door". The idea is that, once the liquor starts flowing, if everybody has their gun with them, nobody will make it out alive. (Which is very, very bad for bar business.)

Anyway, there is a similar truth relating to Infinite, Limitless, Eternal Beings when they go about creating Universes in which to have experience:

They have to leave their infinite power at the door.

Remember, at the eternal level, there is no movement, change or experience. If the Infinite, Limitless Creative Author of the Universe (You) were to project here WITH your gun, I mean with your infinite power, in every time there was a threat, you would automatically go "poof", dissolve everything and be stuck back in boring-ass eternity with nowhere to go and nothing to do.

You had to hide your infinite power. You didn't lose it. You just gave yourself "temporary amnesia" so you could have intense, convincing experience (which, again, requires limitation).

And... guess where you hid it. (I'll tell you in just a bit.)

Along Came Science...

So, back to our story. Pretty much all of the prophets and seers and Masters got burned, crucified or tickled to death for daring to speak the truth of existence.

And then along came science... denying the magic and denying spiritual "truth" and seeking for truth—mostly in places where it ain't.

But science continued to ask and investigate, and eventually created "lenses" for exploration. Big ones—which we aimed further and further "out there" and small ones—which we aimed deeper and deeper "in here."

The small ones became microscopes. And we dove deeper into smallness, trying to find out what it is that things are made of.

Just a few decades ago, basically an eye-blink in time, we found out about these tiny little things that we decided to call "atoms." And we reached the conclusion that atoms are the smallest unit there is. We were told that there is nothing any smaller—and it does not matter if we're talking about gold, lead or hydrogen.

Nope. Atoms were "it."

We were also told that an atom has mass and occupies space.

We were told that it exists.

Jus' Blinkin' Lights

But those darned scientists just couldn't stop asking questions. They developed better and better microscopes. They went down even deeper inside to see what was actually in there. When they finally went inside the electron, much to their surprise, there was nothing there!

Literally—*no-thing* there.

It was all just tiny sub-sub-subatomic little lights blinking in and out of existence that were vibrating at a certain frequency. We *perceived as an electron*, but there was nothing there.

Newtonian physics (formulated into very convincing spells) had us convinced that there is a physical basis to everything. Our senses, as they always do, backed up our spells.

We "knew" that there was a physical universe here. But...

We hadn't been able to find anything physical in the electron, so we figured that the "thing," the "stuff" that was physical, must be inside the nucleus; and so we went inside the nucleus, and there was nothing there either!

Again, it was just these subatomic lights blinking in and out of existence faster than our equipment could measure, going from somewhere (here) to nowhere, as if something were trying to "seem like" it existed.

Quote: "One of the big questions for Quantum Physicists, when we see these particles blinking in and out of existence is whether or not, when the particle disappears, is there a Quantum Physicist 'over there' who sees it appear—and who, when it shows up for us, asks, 'Where did it go?'"—Fred Alan Wolf

This led to the revelation that *the entire universe itself is made up of nothing—a nothing with the ability to show up as everything, which shows up in the form of sub-sub-sub atomic "lights" blinking in and out of existence.*

Wacky s***!

According to the Buddha, arguably one of the greatest teachers of all time—this "blinking in and out of existence" happens at the rate of septillion times per second.

So, chew on that for a moment: The entire universe is non-physical light energy arising and passing away, arising and passing away, a septillion times per second. (1,000,000,000,000,000,000,000,000/sec).

Nothing "Matters"

As Einstein said, *"Concerning matter, we have been all wrong. There is no matter."*

Simply put, everything—everything—EVERYTHING is just light energy blinking in and out of existence.

Close your eyes, take some deep breaths, and allow yourself to expand and take that in…

The ENTIRE Universe is simply light blinking in and out of existence in seeming darkness—and all of it is actually One Limitless Being of Infinite Possibilities. There is no separation. There are no "separate" "things".

It is an Infinite Eternal Being Projecting out of Eternity, into time and space to have an experience.

And You Are That.

Yes.

Allow yourself to breathe deep and feel into that Truth.

Want Some "Even Better News"?

Now here comes some truly magnificent, magical "news!"

Please consider the natural corollary of what we are discussing:

If it is true that:

We are ONE Infinite Eternal Being and

We don't really exist in time and space and

All that we are arises and passes away a septillion times/sec then…

We are actually always existing in a constant state of perpetual Grace! Innocence.

No "sin" or "badness" or "wrong" or "problem"—or disease—or any kind of perceived limitation or obstacle—carries across that septillionth-of-a-second gap… unless *we bring it with us.*

Again:

There is no continuity other than what we think and believe that we know.

Maybe it is time for us to "un-know" a few things.

So, how do we begin to move from "the known" of the Newtonian Addiction to Misery, a world of poison, pain and prisons—to the Level 5 Paradigm of Total Personal Freedom?

At the most radical level, is it possible that we might look out at the Universe and back up far enough and wide enough that we once again see and realize that the entire thing is just light blinking in and out of darkness, not physical at all?

And with no continuity other than what we think we know?

And, if we are willing to give up "knowing," and embrace "not knowing," what might we find?

Perhaps we would discover –

– A Universe of Infinite Possibilities, which is secretly the Embodiment of One Infinite Limitless Being, projecting out of Eternity into Time and Space.

And yes, "Thou art that."

Secrets of a Conscious Creator: On The Universe

If the universe is just lights blinking in and out of existence, then how come my reality feels so real? When I stub my toe on a rock, it hurts. When I bang my hand on this table, it feels hard. What would you say to that?

"Reality is merely an illusion, albeit a very persistent one."
—Albert Einstein

Answer: It only seems so real because we were hypnotized to focus that way, and were put under spells through all the parental, society, cultural, and religious conditioning that we "bought" since birth.

At the "seemingly physical" level of this, the culprit behind spells is the R.A.S., the reticular activating system, inside of your brain. A lot of people are talking about this, but not in the way we are about to.

Inside of your brain you are taking in four million bits of information every second. It comes in through every nerve, your optical system, auditory system, olfactory system, taste, everything.

Every nerve in your entire body comes in and feeds into the reticular activating system which then filters down all of the four million bits into about 2,000 bits.

This is only a tiny fraction of the information available to you, so we are not getting the whole picture of anything, ever. Even more damaging is that we are only getting *the same 2,000 bits* over and over and over and over.

So, what do you think happens when you are only allowed to see the same 2,000 bits over and over and over again?

You begin to think and believe that you "know" something!

We can only believe and achieve what we can conceive of.

If we were brought up to be meat suits, what kind of reality would we be able to conceive of?

If we identified as "minds", what would we be blinded from seeing?

If we are bound by religion, what will be hidden from our sight?

And if we think we are supposed to "be spiritual", what kind of charades will we find ourselves playing?

In each of those scenarios, there will be things we want that we just can't get, because our spells/beliefs/RAS holds the means for "getting it" out of our reach.

Simultaneously, our spells/beliefs/RAS will be busy keeping everything that we don't want continually right there, holding us back.

In each of those scenarios, our reality is dense, and we feel stuck, separate, and powerless.

Yet if we shifted our paradigm to take in the Truth that we are actually Infinite, Limitless Beings, then what kind of reality would open up for us? What would the "physical world" be like for us then? What would we see and be and feel and create that up until now, we have not been able to see and be and feel and create?

We've all heard that we are made in the image of God—with the ability to create universes. (If you see yourself as atheist or agnostic, and don't like the word "God," then just call it energy. Trust me, despite thousands of years of hypnotized people killing each other over whose name and image of God is the correct one, the Eternal Being of Energy just is as it is, and it doesn't care what you or I call it.)

But until we break our spells, our RAS will continue blocking our Infinite Resources, reducing the four million (or so) bits that are available to us in every second down to a couple thousand.

What would open up for you, if you actually lived your true, infinite, eternal identity?

We are going to find out.

In this chapter, we accepted the First Key, and began to shift our Core Paradigm from the scarcity and limitation of the lower 4 paradigms to the Infinite Freedom of the 5th Paradigm.

In the next chapter, we will grasp the 2nd Key…

Secrets of a Conscious Creator: What's the point?

So if everything is just lights blinking in and out of existence, and there's no universe—then what's the point? What even matters?

Answer: Well, I would meet that question with a question. How do you want to feel? I don't concern myself with meaning, I don't concern myself with what matters or doesn't matter, I don't concern myself with intellectual questions about aliens and angels, or any of it. I guide my life on the premise of Infinite, Eternal Being projecting out of eternity into time and space to have experience.

That means that I am here, in this current incarnation, for experience and that means my only concern is—what do I want to experience now?

And what happens when we drop our spells and begin to focus on what we want to experience?

In the moment that we turn, without resistance, to that focus, we bring all of our awareness, "all the wisdom, knowledge, information and power that has ever been and will ever be" to bear on that one single focus.

With that focus, we find that all the resources that we could ever need to assist us are here, ready to empower us to experience only that which we want to experience. Simultaneously, all of the resources are there to help us to deal with and dissolve everything else that might have before gotten in the way.

I personally choose not to wrap up my precious time, energy or focus on theoretical questions that might entertain the mind, but don't really help me to create the life that I want for myself and my family and clients.

**Have a question for me? See what others
have asked and ask your own question at
www.BreakYourSelfHelpAddiction.com/ama.
I want to hear from you.**

Chapter 5

The Second Key: Become Present and Centered in Your Power

"Regulate the breathing, and thereby control the mind."
—BKS Iyengar

Once you've shifted your paradigm, and accepted the unlimited and eternal nature of what you are, then becoming centered in that paradigm becomes the most important thing that you can do.

We're preparing to actually *leverage and utilize* the infinite energy of existence, all the knowledge, information and wisdom that's ever been and will ever be.

All the power that creates all the universe(s)… inexhaustible… is always at our disposal.

We've been blinded to the fact that it is ours—and is us. We were always using it, all along—albeit unconsciously—to create our lives of "more of the same".

Now that we're once again becoming aware of it, we're going to begin aiming and focusing it intentionally.

In order to do it, we must be centered, focused and aligned.

Consider a super-powered fire-hose, running full-blast. It requires three or four burly firefighters to hold, manage and aim. The pressure and power is just too intense for one person.

Well, multiply that power by, well, infinity, and you'll have a "visual" on this idea.

You are able to manage it, but you must be clear and fully present to do so.

There are 2 techniques that I'm going to share with you. You can use these at any time. You can use them all the time. It will actually help you to be centered in your body, in your center of awareness, and in the center of the present moment.

The 5 Layer Breath Technique

Before you begin, I want to offer you a word of encouragement:

This breathing technique, by itself, is actually enough to begin to transform your life and end the cycles of pain, frustration and chronic, unpleasant emotion for you. There is no way that I could overstate or exaggerate this.

The vast majority of people are breathing at a severely inadequate depth, and giving their bodies only a tiny fraction of the life-giving magic and energy of oxygen/air. The effects of this "normal" breathing are truly damaging and devastating in many ways.

For our purposes, the main reason we are advocating this breath technique is because oxygen is the catalyst for fire—including emotional fire. Deep breathing rapidly moves trauma, frozen energy and emotions out of the body. Later, when we get into Spellbreaking, this breathing technique will be one of your greatest allies.

In Hawaii, where I live and conduct my Liberation work, we talk of "mana" which is a spiritual quality considered to have supernatural origin–a sacred impersonal force existing in the universe—an aspect of The One Infinite, Eternal Being.

Among other things, it is the "life force" carried by the breath that brings healing and vitality to the body.

In Hindu philosophy including yoga, Indian medicine, and martial arts, the term is "prana," and refers collectively to all cosmic energy, permeating the Universe on all levels. Prana is often referred to as the "life force" or "life energy".

We are about to harness and leverage some Prana Mana!

Before you begin, I want to bring your awareness to two concepts, both of which can be found at www.BreakYourSelfHelpAddiction. com/breath

1. This breath technique is very basic, but it does assume that you have familiarity with **"Abdominal Breathing"**. If you're not already skilled at Abdominal Breathing, or if you'd like a refresher, watch this super short video before continuing.

2. Most people in modern societies are not familiar with the true functions of the diaphragm or with the full process of breath in the body. This equally short video will help you to get much more out of this practice. **"Diaphragm Awareness Training"**

The 5 Layer Breath Technique, broken down:

Step 1: Breathe with Nasal Inhalation and Mouth Exhalation

First of all, using abdominal breathing, you're going to begin to breathe in through your nose and out through your mouth. As you inhale, bring air all the way down to your belly; and as you exhale, have it leave your belly. You're going to practice that for several breaths.

Step 2: Make Inhalation and Exhalation the Same Duration

The second layer of this breathing technique is to make sure that the duration of your inhale and the duration of your exhale are approximately the same length. We're going to breathe in through the nose, out through the mouth and for about the same duration with each phase.

Step 3: Expand Airflow

The third layer of this technique is to begin to breathe in a little bit more deeply than you normally would and breathe out a little more completely than you normally would. When we breathe in more than usual, we're going to be conscious of our diaphragm, as it comes down and stretches our lungs. When we breathe out, our diaphragm pushes our lungs up higher and pushes more air out.

Step 4: Iron the Breath

The fourth layer of the breathing is that we're going to imagine that we have an iron, like an iron that you would iron your clothes with. We're going to iron over the breath, so that it's smooth and continuous, with no pause or gap in between. So as we breathe in and out, the iron tracks over the breath and irons out all the wrinkles.

In effect, what we have now is a smooth flow of air coming in through the nose and out through the mouth. We have an equal duration of in breath and out breath. We're breathing in a little bit more than usual, causing the diaphragm to go down lower than usual. We're breathing out a little more than usual, causing the diaphragm to come up a little more than usual, removing more air. We can hear it and feel it. And then with the ironing metaphor, we are also making sure that the breath is smooth and continuous, with no gap or pause in between.

Step 5: Bring Love In with A Smile
The fifth layer of the breath is to actually bring a smile of love to your face. You may feel funny or weird or self-conscious as you do this, but it doesn't matter, just try it on anyway!

As you feel the love and you put the smile on your face, you are doing what I consider to be the only two necessary "spiritual practices": smiling and breathing.

Up until now, we have been pretty convinced that the way life works is that things happen, and we get happy and then smile—and there is some truth in that.

Yet it's equally true that those wires also run in reverse. In other words, when you smile, you send the signal to your nervous system— and to the universe—(which is the rest of your body) that all is well, and helps to calm all your systems down, bringing you to a center of resourcefulness.

As you breathe in through the nose, out through the mouth and follow this process, you are adjusting and balancing your nervous system. You're calming your mind, your heart, and your body down.

[Callout] Recap the 5 Steps of Becoming Centered
1. Breathe in through your nose and out through your mouth in slow, easy, even breaths
2. Make the inhalation and exhalation the same duration—breathe in and out the same length
3. Expand your airflow—inhale a little deeper and exhale a little more than you normally would

4. Iron your breath and smooth out the creases, so that your breath is smooth, continuous and without gaps or pauses

5. Bring love in—physically bring a big smile to your face and bring peace to your mind and body.

This will bring you into a more peaceful, calm and resourceful state. At the VERY least, because you're focusing your awareness on the breathing as much as you are, you literally cannot focus as much on those old limiting thoughts and patterns as you were before. Without attention, they begin to deflate like an unplugged inflatable toy.

(These statements are not evaluated or proven by the Food and Drug Administration. (Not sure what food and drugs have to do with breathing…) They have also not been evaluated by the Fraud and Death Administration or any of the possible legal entities on this—or any other—planet. I'm not a lawyer, doctor, astronaut or licensed, bonded breather, so just feel it for yourself. If you are dead or otherwise unable to breathe, please see a doctor. But only if you really want to.) My official legal disclaimer can be found in its appropriate place in this book and on my website.)

GO DEEPER
Want some more help and support? Let me actually walk you through this process on video.

www.BreakYourSelfHelpAddiction.com/breath

The "Past Future Extraction" Technique
The second technique for getting centered is the "Past Future Extraction". If you can do this "on top of", or while doing, the 5 Layer Breath, it is even more powerful.

Remember, there is no past and there is no future—there is only this present moment. Any of the pain and fear that you've had in your past, and any of the fear and anxiety about your future are needless energy drains.

This exercise will completely sever the mind's reliance on the past and future and bring you to a place of complete present awareness. It will catapult you into a more resourceful state and help you to anchor yourself into Presence every time you use it.

Bringing the Past into the Present

Once you're already breathing with the 5 Layer Technique, close your eyes.

In your mind, look into the past and envision just the left side of your body.

With your eyes still closed, look off to the left in front of you.

Imagine that off to the left there is a long line representing the entirety of the past.

Just give it a moment—in your mind's eye, become present to everything that you've ever done or that's ever been done "to you", from this very moment all the way back to the time you were born.

All one long line, going off into the distance.

Now you're going to invite all of your energies, all of the places where you got stuck, all of the areas of frozen-ness, any area of you that might have been engaged in past thoughts, fears or concerns— simply snap them all directly into the present with one strong inhale and then "cannonball" the breath out (make one super strong exhale out of the mouth).

Bringing the Future into the Present

Feel all of yourself coming to this moment now, continue the breathing technique and now look off to the right into your future.

In your mind's eye, become present to any of the worries, concerns or fears that you might have been projecting forward, anything that you believe that's been happening that you think "means" something will happen in the future.

See any worries or concerns projected forward about what might happen, see them in one long line all the way to infinity to your right.

– and then snap the entirety of the future into the present moment with one strong inhale and then "cannonball" the breath out again— with one super strong exhale out of the mouth.

And then relax. Take a few nice, deep breaths and allow yourself to integrate what you just did.

You have just brought more of your energies from past and future "projection" into your present moment. Feel the expanded presence and resources available to you now. (Every time you do this, you will receive deeper, more expansive benefits.)

GO DEEPER

To eliminate confusion and help you get the most out of this ULTRA-powerful technique, please go and watch the super-short video:

www.BreakYourSelfHelpAddiction.com/past-future

Secrets of a Conscious Creator: On Breathing
Question: How can something as simple as breathing change my life?

Answer: Many people are stunned and amazed when they first discover the incredible healing and transformational power of conscious breath. I have come up with an analogy that has helped a lot of people to get this, so that they could integrate it into their lives.

So imagine a problem in your life. Maybe it's a disease or a relationship issue. Maybe it's a money "block" that just keeps coming back over and over again, no matter what you have done to combat it.

In my work, I've discovered that all of these issues arise from frozen energy. Basically, chunks of energy frozen in the physical body. In my intense one-on-one and group Spellbreak work, I actually help people to dissolve those frozen chunks of energy at the root, freeing up tons of "mana"—tons of that vital life force energy, and causing instantaneous, deep, and lasting life transformation.

So, for this example, I'm going to liken this frozen chunk of energy to a sandcastle.

Imagine that, while the tide was out, you have built the best sandcastle in the world. It is tightly packed, compacted, and then re-compacted until it's almost like solid rock. Looks and feels like solid rock—a sandcastle that seems just as hard and impenetrable as a brick.

You might think this sandcastle is indestructible.

And then the tide starts to come in. The mild wash of even the very first wave begins to demolish it. By just the third or fourth wave, it's all just sand again.

All that energy that seemed so stuck and solid, has now returned back to its original formlessness.

In this analogy, the sand sculpture is the traumatic issue and the frozen energy in your body, and the waves are your conscious breath.

As you breathe in and breathe out deeply, bringing in the healing power of oxygenated lifeforce in and out, over and over again, while you're focusing on the feelings of that issue—you are actually, literally dissolving that frozen energy at the roots.

Have a question for me? See what others have asked and ask your own question at www.BreakYourSelfHelpAddiction.com/ama. I want to hear from you.

Chapter 6

The Third Key: Focus on What You Want to Experience

"Change your thoughts and you change your world."
—Norman Vincent Peale

Now that you have begun to shift your core paradigm, now that you are beginning to use your breath to release the frozen chunks of energy that were holding you back, and now that you are have begun to get centered and present in the Level 5 Paradigm, now what?

What flows from the acceptance of the possibility that you are an Infinite, Limitless Being—projecting out of time and space to have an experience?

All of the infinite wisdom, knowledge, information and power that's ever been and that will ever be is flowing out of eternity and into time and space through you.

And you are relearning that you have the full ability to focus all of that infinite energy with your mind.

The wisdom, power and grace that creates universes is your nature. It is at your command.

Up until this moment, you have been creating your life, your world, and your universe unconsciously _out of your spells_. You were unknowingly allowing your inexhaustible flow of infinite power to flow from your spells into manifestation of more of the same.

What would it be like to stop creating by default, and to begin to _consciously focus_ that energy explicitly into that which you want to experience?

I share with my clients and event attendees the Radical Truth of Infinite Intelligence:

1. All of the Knowledge, Wisdom, Information and Power that has ever been and will ever be is flowing to you and through you—at your command.
2. The only thing you cannot do is turn it off. It is going to continue to flow.
3. You've only got 2 choices of what you can do. You can either: a) focus on what you want to experience or b) you can fall into thought.

The Outcome of Falling into Thought

When you fall into thought, you end up doing what the vast majority of us have been doing our entire lives, falling into the improper use of the mind.

We have access to all of the infinite wisdom, knowledge, information, and power flowing into us at all times like a fire hose, and yet instead of directing it to consciously create the life of our dreams, we are used to just letting it spray wild and willy-nilly all over the place—and beat the hell out of us in the process.

When you fall into thought, you look at "what is" (or your "spellbound" interpretation of what is) and you think something like, "Aw, s***... *this?*"

Then you refer to memory and you look at all the things that that reminds you of—the things we have already associated unconsciously with what is in front of us. And we give a second, "Aw, s***... *this* reminds me of *that!*"

With our focus on "what is" and "what was", we are unconsciously aiming the "Infinite Firehose of Creation Power" to spray into the formation and creation of "more of the same", and *that's why things keep repeating.*

Whenever we get triggered or begin to feel an unpleasant emotion around anything that's going on, the general habit is to think "Aw, s***, 'this' means 'that'". The minute that that happens, know that you've fallen into thought again.

You have fallen from Infinite Being and gotten stuck in your mental body, and you're going to be completely resource-less.

On the other hand, when you focus on what you want to experience, you actually take control of "The Firehose of Infinite Creation Power" through the lens of your mind and begin to consciously direct it (or "aim" it) into forming and manifesting what you want.

Focusing on What You Want to Experience

You've already mastered falling into thought, so....

Instead of doing more of that, I invite you to grasp the reins of your mind and aim that amazing "lens" to intentionally focus all the infinite wisdom, knowledge, information and power that's ever been and will ever be directly into what it is that you want to experience.

Now how, exactly, do you do that?

It's actually as simple as asking a question.

Well, not just any question. Many questions are downright destructive.

To begin to aim the Infinite Power consciously, we are going to ask a Quantum Question.

We will discuss Quantum Questions more in the next chapter. For now, we want to get you into action with a basic understanding.

A QQ is a tool that literally aims and directs and focuses all of the infinite wisdom, knowledge, information and power that has ever been and ever will ever be—directly into the creation of what you are thinking/feeling about.

When you ask a Quantum Question, you do not go into your head and try to "figure out" the answers. Rather, you tune in and "feel into" the energies that arise in response to the question.

(You might want to read that again.)

An ideal Quantum Question to ask when you want to focus on what you want to experience would be: "What would I like to experience now?"

Let's take a moment, and take that in—and let's consider our first three keys:

Key 1: Consider the Level 5 Paradigm: Infinite Being Projects out of Eternity into Time and Space To Have Experience. I Am That. And it all arises and passes away a septillion times a second, so I am in a state of perpetual grace. There is no continuity other than what I think and believe that I know.

Key 2: Close your eyes and breathe deeply in through the nose and out through the mouth.

Make the duration of inhale and exhale the same.

Breathe just a bit more deeply in and out than usual.

Iron out the wrinkles and really smooth out the breath.

Smile and Feel the Love.

Key 3: Now, from inside of your body, not your head, ask yourself that question slowly, out loud:

"What would I like to experience now?"

And feel into it. Feel your mind and your energy all calibrating and focusing itself to align with that question.

Don't try to figure it out, don't let the mind get "realistic," practical or logistical, rather—feel into the energy of that question.

Now that you have felt into that question, allow yourself to ask again, and reflect on the actual *feeling* that you want to experience.

For example, you might think, "Oh I would really like to feel happy right now."

Let that be enough for now- because the magic of focusing on what you want to experience aims that energy directly towards the flow of that feeling and experience that you want to experience.

Now, we've always been convinced that we want (and need) the house, the car, the money, that great lover, that partner, etc., but the truth is that we actually don't.

As pointed out by many of the greatest teachers on the planet (and off):

What we actually want is the *feeling* we believe that we will have when we have the thing or experience.

If you allow yourself to think "Oh, what I really want is that house," you immediately put yourself in opposition to all of the beliefs and rules and values that have been keeping the house out of your experience! (what you think other people will think, where you will get the money, etc…)

There are no "things" here. It is all energy. When you think of the "thing", you switch all of your related spells back on.

So instead of focusing on the "thing" that you think you want, focus on the *feeling* and *experience* that you want to have.

Here is the most magical aspect of this incredibly powerful third Key:

When you focus your energy in this way with a Quantum Question, a few literally magical things happen:

The energies of the universe will now flow into the feelings that you want to have—

You will be guided by those feelings to the exact actions to take that will bring you to it —

You simultaneously become a magnet, literally attracting it to yourself—

Take a moment and read the last few sentences again. Then, let's get ready for the next key…

Secrets of a Conscious Creator: On Focus
"What if I don't know what I want?"

Answer: Great! You are in the perfect place!

Would you like to feel more love? More peace? More confidence? More clarity or certainty?

Just feel that feeling. As you feel it fully, it will lead and inspire you to the next question or action that will bring you clarity about what you DO want.

Have a question for me? See what others
have asked and ask your own question at
www.BreakYourSelfHelpAddiction.com/ama.
I want to hear from you.

Chapter 7

The Fourth Key: Clear the Past (Spellbreaks)

"Humans believe so many lies because we aren't aware. We ignore the truth or we just don't see the truth. When we are educated, we accumulate a lot of knowledge, and all that knowledge is just like a wall of fog that doesn't allow us to perceive the truth, what really is."

—Don Miguel Ruiz

N ow that we have begun to accept the Level 5 Paradigm, we want to fully shift into harmony with it.

We want to stop re-creating more of "what is" by default, and we want to experience more of what we WANT to experience. So, we are choosing to become fully Present and Centered, bringing our full resources of the Level 5 Paradigm into The Present Moment so we can effectively take the next step:

We choose to Focus on What We Want To Experience.

When you begin to focus on what you want to experience, you actually may find yourself moving directly towards it, and you might find it, actually—gasp!—happening for you!

There are going to be times when it's going to be very easy, even effortless!

And as you do this more and more, it's going to become easier and easier.

However, as I had said at the end of the last chapter, when you begin to go after something you really want, you will very often find your pre-existing related spells (and associated pains and chronic emotions) rearing their ugly heads and rising up between you and the experience you desire.

This leads us to a crucial, critical point:

Honey, Where Did I Leave My Infinite Power?

In the last chapter, in the "Creation Myth" section, I finished by pointing out that, like the redneck bar patron leaving his gun at the door, an Infinite, Eternal Being has to leave Its Infinite Power at the door in order to have a "convincing" experience of limitation.

You didn't lose it. You are not powerless. You just hid it.

And I told you that I was going to reveal to you where you hid it.

Ready?

You hid it in the ONLY place you would never look: Inside of everything you fear and hate or strongly dislike.

All of those "bad" things and "scary" things and "yucky" people.

Remember, when you "get" that you are the only one here, you have to "get" that everything is actually YOU. There are no "external forces" to harm or tease or torment you. And there are no "external" things—including people.

It really is ALL You.

Everything that you like, love, and appreciate is already close to you—in your "comfort zone".

Everything that you avoid is the secret hiding place of your Infinite Power.

And those things BITE. They hurt. They smell. They are scary. They are sleazy, slimy and repulsive. They are threatening and yucky.

Well, they appear that way to your spells.

And when you begin to move towards what you want to experience, you come face to face with everything you ever placed between "yourself" and "that" (which you are sure is "not yourself").

And it comes, again, with all of the chronic unpleasant emotion associated with the spells.

That's when it's time to do a Spellbreak!

There are three major types of Spellbreaks:

1. **Basic Self-Spellbreak**
2. **Full Self-Spellbreak**
3. **Guided Spellbreak**

In form, they are similar.

In function, they are radically different. In truth, compared to a Guided Spellbreak, the self-spellbreaks are very limited, for reasons we will discuss in a moment. However, they can make the difference between heaven and hell in the moment.

Many people who get access to my book or free videos immediately know that this work is "for them" and that they want to investigate stepping to the next level with me, either 1-on-1 or in a group, online or here at my "Transformation to Liberation" Private Retreats in Hawaii.

If that is you, then you are going to experience one or more Guided Spellbreaks with me. Whether you feel that is true for you or not, I want you to have every resource possible for your own liberation.

Before we get into the how's, let's get totally clear on the why's:

Why Spellbreaks Are Necessary

As I said, there will be times when you will find yourself using the first three keys and just flowing with awesomeness.

Very often, though, the minute you begin to step towards what you want, you will find *everything you ever put between yourself and that showing up*, seemingly with the purpose of blocking your progress.

This experience can be intense. And the "bigger" your desire and the "bigger" the thing you are going after, the more intense the resistance.

And the more emotional-intensity carried in your spell, the more painful it will be to face it or experience it being triggered.

It will be helpful for you to get your mind "on your side", helping and supporting you with your desired outcomes, so let's get a clear understanding of exactly what is happening.

When you step towards what you want, you are doing a few things all-at-once:

1. You are creating change—which scares the hell out of your mind/RAS

2. You are moving towards something new—which also scares the mind/RAS

3. You are also going after something which, in all probability, is tangled up with multiple layers of beliefs and spells—which

is going to stir up all of the emotions associated with the experiences during which the spells were created

This is a critical point: When we are triggered, the emotion that was tied up in the spell will be triggered. It will be one of our clues and allies. It will be the focal point we will aim our awareness at first.

1. Basic Self-Spellbreak

This first Self-Spellbreak can be used anytime, as a sort of "quick remedy" to getting yourself quickly out of a mildly unresourceful emotional place.

It is in the form of what we had earlier referred to as a "Quantum Question." Recall that a Quantum Question is a tool that literally aims and directs and focuses all of the infinite wisdom, knowledge, information, and power that has ever been—and will ever be—directly into the creation of what you are thinking/feeling about.

When you ask a Quantum Question, you do not go into your head and try to "figure out" the answers. Rather, you tune in and "feel into" the energies that arise in response to the question.

When you begin to focus on what you want to experience and you notice resistance in the form of an undesired emotion—anger, sadness and/or fear—you can use this ultra-simple, yet deceptively powerful Quantum Question:

"How would I prefer to feel about this?"

And allow the question to resonate through your whole being...

In many cases, you will have a release and experience relief from this alone!

Why? Because you were unconsciously experiencing the unpleasant emotion of the spell and unconsciously focusing your energy and awareness there. The question itself is an effective wedge between your mind and your infinite being and it breaks the pattern very near the roots.

When the question alone doesn't bring relief, take the next step:

Feel the unpleasant emotion and ask if it is anger, sadness or fear. (If you get any other answer, you are still stuck in your mind. You can easily move your focus back to your emotional body by asking again: "What emotion am I really feeling behind this story? Is it anger, sadness or fear?)

Once you know, ask your Quantum Question again:

"How would I prefer to feel about this?" You will begin to feel the opposite emotion from the one you were stuck in. If it was fear, you'll begin to feel confident, certainty and safety—peace.

If it was sadness, you will feel happiness/joy arising.

If it was anger, you will find loving peace arising.

This Basic Self-Spellbreak is the go-to tool for when the unpleasant emotion and resistance are subtle.

Now, let's look at the detailed steps of this practice.

The Steps of the Basic Self-Spellbreak:

1. Recall the essence of the Level 5 Paradigm
2. Ask, "What emotion am I feeling in relationship to this topic?" (Anger, sadness and/or fear)
3. Take a few 5-Layer Breaths and Become Centered and Present.
4. Tune into your body and ask, "How would I prefer to feel about this?"
5. Feel your body tune into the question and feel it respond with the feeling. It will usually be the approximate "opposite" feeling. (If you were feeling fear, you will likely want to feel confidence, certainty, peace, trust or safety.)
6. Feeeeeeeeeel that feeling.

7. Anchor and stabilize the feeling by asking, "When is this feeling available?", feeling the answer and then asking, "How much more of this feeling is available to me now?"

2. The Complete Self-Spellbreak

In the Complete Self-Spellbreak, you will delve deeper and you will more thoroughly dissolve the issue/spell that is blocking you, at its very roots. It is recommended to be in a safe, quiet, private, and unrushed space to do this so that you can be fully present.

Think about the issue that is blocking you. Really reflect on it.

You're going to begin to feel an emotion arise, and you're going to ask yourself a simple question –

"What am I really feeling about this—is this anger, sadness or fear?"

That question is going to bring you out of the universe that's seemingly "out there". It will bring you out of your "outer universe" focus, beyond your mental body and directly into your emotional body.

Once you give awareness to the anger, sadness or fear, you're going to consciously feel the emotion, and you're going to allow yourself to feel it as completely as you can.

**Hint: The more powerfully and fully you allow yourself to really feel that emotion, the more efficiently and effectively you're going to dissolve the very roots of it. It is literally going to dissolve and depart from your body.

When the emotion comes on nice and strong, you're going to ask a second question:

"Where am I feeling the strongest sensation in my body?"

You will feel either a tightness, a tension, a constriction, a pressure, or even a pain.

Here's the key: Separate away from ideas about what it is and simply call it a sensation. **Hint: Forget what you "know"**.

What to do:

1. As you feel that sensation in your body, take 2 fingers and place them gently on your skin at the place where that feeling resonates the strongest. Move your fingers gently around to find the sharpest center of that sensation.

2. Rest your two fingers at the central point of that sensation where you can feel it the most clearly and intensely, and begin the deep breathing technique.

3. For the next few minutes or however long it takes, you're going to literally dive your awareness directly into that physical sensation. Imagine standing on the side of a pool and actually diving straight into the physical sensation. Move your awareness directly and deeply into the physical sensation. You want to move your awareness to the point of such focus on the sensation that everything else—emotions, thoughts, memories, everything—disappears.

The key to this process is to become ONE with the sensation—and then flowing your awareness, which is LOVE, directly into the sensation to dissolve it at the roots.

When the sensation is gone down to zero in intensity, the issue is gone and your life WILL be changed.

When you feel that the sensation is gone, you can test it by bringing up the issue and thinking the thoughts that seemed so upsetting at the start. You'll be stunned and amazed to realize that the issue is gone.

GO DEEPER

If you find yourself having a difficult time moving into the physical sensation, you can go right now and learn how to master moving inside your body and feeling the physical sensations. **www. BreakYourSelfHelpAddiction.com/Spellbreaks**

Some people find this easier than others. Now that you're back and you know how to dive into that physical sensation, let's do it. Once you dive into that physical sensation, your job becomes very, very simple.

- You have allowed the issue to come up in your life.
- You have found the emotion that's behind it and now you've moved beyond the emotion into the physical sensation that's underneath it all.
- You're going to feel that physical sensation with all of your power of awareness.
- You're going to feel it fully, from 50%, 70%, 80%, 90% until you reach a 100% of focus.
- At a 100%, you will have become one with the physical sensation in all its intensity.

It can get "uncomfortable" and "confronting" and "intense." But just stay with it and allow yourself to really feel the emotions, and stay focused on the physical sensation while breathing deep and allowing your powerful life force breath to go through your whole body.

You're giving it all of your attention, which means that you're giving it all of your love, which means you are now feeling the things and emotions that you had been avoiding, that had been blocking your energy, for who knows how many years or decades. So surround those things and emotions with your deep breath, your full conscious attention, your powerful unconditional love...

There is a powerful idea that we have not fully dealt with that becomes crucial to understand at this point:

This sensation is the physical effect of one or more frozen chunks of energy in your body. These frozen chunks of energy were created from early childhood trauma.

Something shocking or painful happened, and we gasped, and a part of our lifeforce (mana—prana) got frozen in our body.

You've been unknowingly at the mercy of this spell from that moment forward.

And, now, by focusing 100% of your full love and awareness INTO that which you had been avoiding, you are literally dissolving that frozen chunk of energy. As you do, the issue related to that begins to release its charge.

As you do that, you will feel energy, lifeforce flowing back in and returning to your body. The resources that had been frozen since that traumatic childhood moment start becoming available to you again and returning to your mental, physical and emotional bodies all at once.

**Hint: It's helpful to tune in every once in a while and ask a question, "If this physical sensation was at 100% at its most intense, what percentage is it at now?"

You will feel the emotional intensity, issue and physical sensation diminishing on its way to dissolving, and your job is to stay with it as completely as you possibly can while it dissolves down to 0.

You'll find it very helpful to maintain the 5-Layer Breathing Technique that we had shared earlier in Step 2.

As it dissolves to 0, allow yourself to continue to breathe deep and lay quietly, and integrate the new healing and transformation that has taken place. Allow yourself to bless yourself and embrace a new reality without that issue holding you back any longer.

What infinite possibilities are now open for you?

3. Guided Spellbreaks

I've got to be radically honest with you: Self-Spellbreaks can be fairly difficult. The more powerful the issue, charge and spell, the more intensely difficult the ability to hold yourself together for a Spellbreak.

To hold 100% of your energy and attention, and especially upon an issue that you're feeling triggered or traumatized by, without someone experienced "holding the container" and guiding you can be a big challenge.

Reflect on the reality that you've been living at the mercy of these spells, having them direct your mind and behaviors, and that you've been avoiding these issues and emotions for years, maybe decades, (maybe your entire life).

You came into this universe as the Ultimate Ninja Master of Creating Limitation, and you've spent a decent number of revolutions around our star in this present body practicing the avoidance of these things!

It would be quite understandable that you may require support to help you break their power over you.

Further, the mind is blind to its own blind-spots—so it's helpful and often necessary to have an objective 3rd party to help you see what you might not be able to see.

I've provided the steps here because I want to give you the most powerful resources possible. Still, most people find that it's a whole lot easier, and a lot more powerful and effective, to have the Spellbreak done "for them" by someone who is expert at holding the space and helping them to stay present and focused.

Fortunately, I know the guy who invented the process, and he could possibly help you with that. ;-)

GO DEEPER

SEE A LIVE SPELLBREAK at:
www.BreakYourSelfHelpAddiction.com/Spellbreaks.

If you're presently experiencing something severe that you want help with, there are options for private 1-on-1, work with me. At the end of this book, I'll tell you about those options.

For now, for whatever you're experiencing, be present with it. Feel it. Stay the course and keep reading, and we will see where you're at by the end of the book.

**Have a question for me? See what others
have asked and ask your own question at
www.BreakYourSelfHelpAddiction.com/ama.
I want to hear from you.**

Chapter 8

The Fifth Key: Become the Master

"The only true wisdom is in knowing you know nothing."
—Socrates

Before we take the Fifth Key in hand, let's quickly recap the first four **Keys to Total Personal and Financial Freedom:**

- Key One: Shift your CORE paradigm
- Key Two: Become Present and Centered In Your Power
- Key Three: Focus On What You Want to Experience
- Key Four: Clear the Past and Recapture Your Power

And now we are on **Key Five: Become the Master.**

Now you have the foundation and the tools to begin to live from the Level Five Paradigm.

It is time for me to invite you to master the *consistent focusing of your infinite power to embody conscious creation on every level and truly Become the Master of Your Life.*

I'm going to give you some tools to help you do that, right now.

Self-Love Is EVERYTHING

The first point I want to make is that it really is all about Self-Love. Now, I don't know about you, but I have been hearing for many years that self-love is the real key, the secret.

"You can't love anyone until you love yourself."

"No one can love you more than you love yourself".

Things like that.

But nowhere could I find a clear and comprehensive and comprehensible description of WHAT self-love is or HOW to do it.

In this section I'm going to give you the basics of how to begin really, truly LOVING yourself. Not "giving or getting the feelings of love". But the actual verb-sense. "Doing" self-love.

Self-love is nice. Sweet. Powerful. Magical.

But when you realize that the Universe is your true Self, it is *everything*.

Conscious Communication

The first ultra-powerful tool is "conscious communication".

This is a huge topic in itself—enough for another book. In my work with clients, we delve deeply into this—and we experience massive miracles as we apply it.

In this book, I want to give you the core essentials and I'll do that in the form of three principles:

1. **Speak From Love**
2. **Speak Problems In The Past**
3. **Listen With Full Presence**

1. Speak From Love

First, we're going to learn to speak from—and with—love for yourself and love for others.

When you prepare to speak, first become very conscious of your desired outcome.

In other words, reflect before you open your mouth.

Consider your language and how you want to experience yourself, others and your world.

We now know that the Universe is You and You are the Universe. If you are not engaging with love towards everything in the Universe, then you are not loving yourself. And vice versa!

From this moment forward, never deprecate yourself or put yourself—or others—down. You will speak about yourself (all of you) gently, lovingly, and compassionately.

2. Speak Problems In The Past

From this moment onwards, speak about your "problems" in the past tense. Understand that when you say, "I have 'x-disease'", or "I always screw up 'y'", or "I'm such a 'z'", you are literally commanding the entire Universe (which is your body) to carry out and perpetuate the command.

From now on, create the life of your dreams by saying all of these things truthfully, by putting them where they belong—in the past.

Move from: "I can't do x" to -

"Up until now, I could not do X"

Move from: "I freeze in front of people" to -

"Up until now, I felt nervous in front of people."

Move from: "I have cancer" to -

"**Up until now,** I had the symptoms of what many refer to as cancer."
In short, you're going to speak the truth.

It is actually a lie to say, "I am _____", or "I have _____", because you can only know what you've experienced up until this moment. Do you **really** know if that condition or limitation will continue into the future? Do you really want to consciously carry it forward into the future with unconscious languaging?

Here's an interesting idea—your brain's awareness of the present is actually 80 milliseconds in the past. Did you know that? So in truth, you cannot know that you still have it, because your mind only knows what happened 80 milliseconds ago.

In a reality where the universe is blinking in and out of existence a septillion times per second, 80 milliseconds is a long time! Be here now. ;-)

When we talk about conscious communication, do not make the mistake of thinking that I am trying to get you to "speak positively" or that we are just "cleaning up our language".

Those ideas are Level 2 Paradigm parlor tricks that give the illusion of "being positive".

This conscious communication tool goes to the roots of our manifestation processes in a powerful and magical way.

Remember that point I keep relentlessly making over and over about "continuity". Now, it is going to shine in its full brilliance in your awareness. Consider this in the light of what we are talking about here:

**There is no continuity other than what
we think and believe that we know.**

When you speak problems in the present and future, (i.e.: "I do", "I am", "I have" or "I always"), you are re-creating them and you are perpetuating the "illusion of problems" on that topic. You're reinforcing "what you think and believe you know".

From now on, speak the profound, life-changing truth.

Interpret those seeming "problems" as existing in the past. You'll be amazed to find that this interpretation moves them out of your present and opens you back up to infinite possibilities.

When you know "what is", and affirm "what is", you freeze the Infinite Energy of Creation into "more of what is".

When you release "knowing", you open the doors for the Infinite Energy of Creation to flow back into Infinite Possibilities.

3. Listen With Full Presence

Another big part of the Conscious Communication is listening to yourself and others with Presence. The best way that I can illustrate this is to share it in the form that I share it with my own children:

- "Are you listening, with Eyes, Ears and Heart?"
- "Are you feeling the Heart of the other person?"
- "Are you seeking to understand?"

By listening to yourself and others with presence, you can begin to create some amazing intimacy and magic in all your relationships. This presence will allow you to begin to consciously create the relationships and deep connections of your dreams…

In addition to conscious communication with others, the next tool of Becoming the Master might be called "Seeing Truth". We're going to call it:

Adopting Blessed Perception

Another powerful tool to be a Master of your own life, is to shift your perception to what has been called, "Blessed Perception." (The perception that everything that occurs is a gift—a blessing.)

Instead of living a life by default or being a victim, and feeling powerless at the effects of others or circumstances ("external forces"), as we embrace the Level 5 Paradigm, I invite you to take full responsibility of your life and adopt "Blessed Perception."

In Blessed Perception, I accept that I am an infinite, unlimited energy projecting out of eternity into time and space to have experience.

There are no "external forces" that could, or would have reason to, hurt or harm or punish me.

As an infinite, unlimited, indivisible, complete, eternal, perfect Energy beyond right and wrong, nothing bad can happen, nothing good can happen, nothing better or worse can happen, nothing positive or negative can actually really happen.

All that happens is just what happens, and because it is ALL Me, *it can only be happening **for** me.*

So instead of interpreting life events as happening TO me, I choose to interpret all events as happening *FOR* me.

I Am the One here.

I Am. My highest self is the only one here.

It's all happening for me by my choice—though I may not remember consciously WHY in this moment.

Sometimes, I may not be able to see how that is true, but I am *willing* to see it.

I am willing to be open and curious.

I am willing to stop, breathe, "not know," and ask the Quantum Questions –

- "How is this FOR me?"
- "How did I create/attract this?"
- "How is this the absolute best thing that could happen for me right now?"
- "How is this blessing me right now?"
- "What are the blessings I can harvest from this?"

This is what I mean by "adopting blessed perception." It will change your life.

Now that we have begun to "Consciously Communicate", and "Adopt Blessed Perception", it is time to:

Reinvent Your Environment

Another crucial tool to be a Master in your own life, is to reinvent your environment. Everything surrounding you is probably set up according to an old, limited paradigm. We want to transform that into an environment that anchors in and calls you consistently more fully towards and into the Level 5 Paradigm.

You're probably not going to go out today and rearrange the poles on the planet, but what you can do is—you can make your bathroom a place of love.

You can make your kitchen a place of love.

You can make your workspace a place of love.

You can actually make your mirrors a place of love, and—maybe most fun:

You can make your bedroom, literally, in every sense, into a place of love.

Here's what I recommend. Write out "I love you" notes and stick them all over your house, especially on your mirrors.

Make the wallpaper on your phone and on your desktop out of an image that speaks to your heart and soul. Maybe it's a love note to yourself, or perhaps it's a picture of you smiling the biggest smile of your life with the words "I love you" super-imposed over it.

You can also begin to use essential oils and/or candles around your home.

Find one or two scents that you absolutely adore and when you wake up in the morning, put those in places you're going to be frequenting for that day.

Take time, every day, to actually stop at the bathroom mirror and look into your beautiful eyes and speak to yourself lovingly. You could say something like, "I love you. I care about you. I forgive you. When you did those unconscious things in the past, you were doing your best and I'm letting you off the hook. I love you so much."

Those few seconds can change your life beyond your wildest imaginings—and the more you do it, the more profound the effects will be.

Another profound tool that we practice in Hawai'i is Ho'opono'pono. We say to others and say to ourselves:

"I'm sorry.

Please forgive me.

Thank you.

I love you."

Being willing to say these simple, profound expressions of love towards ourselves and each other can help to clear pain from the past—and cultivate intimacy in the present.

Each of these practices will change your life. Together, they will move you into Heaven on earth. What other ways could you consciously create your environment so that it calls you to your Infinite Self? I encourage you to make a list and act on it—starting now.

Summary of the 5 Keys

These are the 5 essential keys to stepping into life as Conscious Creator:

- **Key One: Shift Your Core Paradigm to The Level 5 Paradigm**
- **Key Two: Become Present and Centered in Your Paradigm**
- **Key Three: Focus On What You Want to Experience**
- **Key Four: Clear The Past And Recapture Your Power**
- **Key Five: Become the Master**

You will find this sequence to be something of a spiral more than a linear progression. In other words, you will find it necessary to revisit the paradigm repeatedly, many times per day.

As you do, you'll find it helpful to take a few of those magical breaths to help you focus more purely on what you want to experience. As you begin to focus on what you desire, you will almost always find "the stuff" coming up to be resolved, loved and dissolved.

The challenge and opportunity of this is significant.

And that is the topic of the next chapter.

Secrets of a Conscious Creator: On Disease
I have a disease or a medical condition. Can this work help me?

"The disease is never fatal, but accepting the diagnosis often is."
—Brian Ridgway

Answer: If you honestly reflect on the concepts of this book, and if you pay special attention to the implications of Chapter 8, The Level 5 Paradigm, you'll discover something profound—**there is actually no such thing as disease.**

We are actually infinite, unlimited beings, projecting out of eternity into time and space to have experience; and the entire Universe is blinking in and out of existence a septillion times per second.

In that Universe, there is no room for disease.

Disease is a manufactured idea. The "system of institutionalized energies" known as "the medical system" has decided to create a set of rules, logical arguments and so-called facts that gives them a monopoly on "medical diagnosis, treatment and options". It allows them to string together any group of symptoms, give it a name (i.e. disease, condition, health issue), and then profit by prescribing a solution for it.

Although, I'm not a doctor, or maybe *because* I'm not a doctor, I can tell you this:

Many times I have worked with a client who had been told that they had a health condition (ranging from the simplest, minor ailment, all the way up to life threatening, fatal, terminal, supposedly "incurable" conditions) and had believed it.

And yet in one, or a few, session(s) with me, the entire condition dismantled itself and dissolved—in the light of their acceptance of their awareness of the Level 5 Paradigm.

One of my favorite quotes is by Indian philosopher and teacher, Jiddu Krishnamurti: "In truth, we can never solve any of our problems. We can only outgrow them".

What does that mean—to outgrow our problems?

It means that at a certain level of seeing, we perceive a problem.

At that level, our thoughts (and all the things that we think and believe that we know) perpetuate as that problem—that condition.

The minute that we allow an insight to arise that is larger, which transcends or eclipses that which we thought that we believed that we knew, then that thing can no longer stand—at which point it literally dissolves and disappears.

The brick-solid sandcastle becomes.... once again.... sand.

Disease obviously does not exist in the Level 5 Paradigm.

So, often, when a person lets that Paradigm in, their "disease" no longer exists.

GO DEEPER

One of my clients, Erica, had scoliosis. Well, according to the first four paradigms, she did.

For 30 years, she had 3 curves in her spine and had difficulty breathing. "Everyone knows" that there is no cure and no real treatment for scoliosis. But when we spent an hour together, and she followed my "strange" idea to really reflect on the Level 5 Paradigm, it was gone.

Hear it from her here: http://www.breakyourselfhelpaddiction. com/Erica

Have a question for me? See what others
have asked and ask your own question at
www.BreakYourSelfHelpAddiction.com/ama.
I want to hear from you.

At this point, I've given you everything I can give you, in one book, to help you break your self-help addiction, assist you to realize that you are not broken, and give you the keys to begin creating the body, health, business, wealth, relationships, life and world of your dreams.

I've given you everything, in one book, that I can—except for a necessary warning. You've done enough of the endless loop of hope>purchase>disappointment of self-help junkiedom.

We gotta make absolutely sure that you don't do it again.

Chapter 9
Don't F*** This One Up

"…and I awaken to find that my only tormentor all along is that part of myself left over from yesterday."
—Unknown

Note: *The rest of this book will be a combination of review and expansion. We will revisit several of the points made in previous chapters while bringing in new light and new ideas.*

Too many courses and programs have already "failed" you. In this chapter, I'm going to give you fair warning of what is going to happen when you set this book down, so you can be prepared—and so you can keep moving forward into ever-more of the experience you really want.

First, let's do a super-fast recap of everything we have covered so far:

1. You, like so many, are ready and willing to accept the possibility—and eventually, the reality—that you are an Infinite, Limitless Being; that Infinite Possibilities are truly yours at all times.

2. You, again, like so many others, have investigated and tried multiple approaches to self-help and personal development without reaching the level of freedom and ease you desire.

3. In your continued intention to create the ultimate life of freedom and ease, you have now encountered the Level 5 Paradigm and the Theory of Constraints (TOC).

4. The Level 5 Paradigm confirms that you are It.

5. The TOC, as applied to "awakening and consciousness" states: Focusing on the Law of Attraction, Consciousness/Awakening and Money/Business/Success courses, programs, seminars, practices, procedures, tools and tactics is less-than-optimal—or nearly pointless—until you uncover and eliminate your Primary Core Constraint.

6. Once you find and dissolve your Primary Core Constraint, you will be free to evolve and expand into your infinite powers at lightning speed.

7. Once you find and dissolve that Primary Core Constraint, all of the previous efforts, learnings and investments you have made will be activated—and multiplied.

8. You are facing the surprising truth that you, like everyone around you, are dealing with an equally surprising Core Constraint: the Core Paradigm of Newtonian Physics (the idea that you are a separate "meatsuit in a machine" driven by fate and "external forces").

9. Now, maybe for the first time, you can see that there is actually nothing wrong with you, that you are NOT broken, and that the "problem" was in the programming/spells you received (and

in the incomplete personal development materials you studied and learned)—not in YOU.

10. You now see the critical importance of a Core Paradigm Shift and have been given the 5 keys to begin to make that shift and integrate it into your life.

This leads to some pretty serious awesomeness:

You are now in the position to begin to focus all of the Wisdom, Knowledge, Information and Power that has ever been—and will ever be—into the creation of the body, health, business, wealth, relationships, life and world of your dreams.

Pretty awesome, isn't it?

It is, and at the same time, it shines a light on a potentially awkward realization.

I can best introduce you to this with 2 targeted questions:

1. Do most people consistently go after what they REALLY want? Or do they passively and reactively live their lives accepting the cards that "fate" deals them?

2. If we are all secretly infinite beings, **why do so few of us go for what we really want?**

I'll tell you why—it is because we learned that when we do, it f*** hurts!

The awkward truth is that the reason why we don't go for what we really, really want is because *every time we did, we got our asses kicked!*

And, now that you have become a fledgling Conscious Creator, you are about to begin walking directly towards the things you want to experience. And when you do, you will come face to face with everything you placed between yourself and that.

I want to prepare you for it.

A Periphery of Invisible Stop Signs

First, though, let's look at how we learned to *not* go for what we want:

- As babies, when we reached out and touched the shiny metal thingy, it burned us!
- As toddlers, when we went exploring and crawled off the edge of the bed/couch/chair and fell on our heads, it hurt!
- When we trusted daddy to be there, sometimes we cried and he didn't instantly show up.
- We asked mommy for that thing at the store and she said no.
- When we reached for it, she smacked our hand.
- As we got a little older, we just loved to sing.
- And when we sang, someone close to us said we sounded like a rat in a blender.
- When we tried our hand at comedy and told our first joke, and…. crickets.

Throughout childhood, our asking and wanting (our seeking for EXPERIENCE) expanded—and so did the pain.

The number 1 word most of were given in response to our asking was: "No."

Then, as we got older and our explorations expanded further still, we ran into an endless stream of more advanced "no's." Parents, priests, preachers, teachers, authorities of all stripes told us not to pursue many of our desires and interests.

Brilliant sayings were handed to us in response to our requests. Things like, "Who do you think you are?", "Do you think money grows on trees?", "You don't really want to do THAT, do you?" and "You selfish little brat!"

And the outcome of all of these pains and "no"s?

We unconsciously spent a lifetime creating something that many personal development experts and coaches call a "Comfort Zone." In conventional self-help and coaching, a comfort zone is the range of "what you have now" and it pretty much excludes "everything you want and are afraid (uncomfortable) to pursue."

The comfort zone is surrounded by a wall made up of "Invisible Stop Signs" that only our RAS sees.

This comfort zone and all of the stop signs are "the chain" holding us in place.

Based on all of our programming and conditioning to these "pains and nos," our RAS has developed an automatic set of responses that is ready to "engage the chain", the minute we take a first step towards what we want.

By reading to this point, you have self-identified as one who is ready and willing to break that chain and make the move into your "desired experience".

In my last several years of helping thousands of people to make that move, I've done hundreds of Private and Group Spellbreaks to help people dissolve "the stuff" that came up when they did. And I can tell you, from experience, what you are up against:

The Old "You" Is "Against" You

Let's put this in the light of The Level 5 Paradigm:

There is actually only One Infinite Being here, and that Being is disguised as the Universe—and as you.

You are the Only One Here.

Every seeming "thing" is actually the same energy as you and, in truth, <u>it IS you</u>.

It is emanating from and through you as you emerge from the Eternal into Time and Space.

Therefore, everything you want to experience is already you, in you and emanating from you.

And, amazingly, all seeming obstacles to what you want are actually you, in you and emanating from you.

So, when you begin to focus on what you really want to experience, you begin to come face to face with everything that you have ever placed between yourself and that.

We've already addressed this, but let's become even more clear with a question:

"How did I get all of that stuff between me and what I want?"

At the spiritual/mental levels, we created, learned and mastered our Spells.

At the physical level, we trained our RAS in patterns to help us stay "safe."

We learned that spiders were scary and bad (arachnophobia) and we have avoided them ever since.

We learned that heights are terrifying (acrophobia) and we have missed out on the beauty of high places ever since.

We learned that men are lying asses (jerkophobia) or that we can't trust women (bitchophobia), or that salespeople are all liars (sleazeophobia), etc., and so we put up all of these walls up between ourselves and what we want.

And now, as you step forward, you will see that it appears that everything you built is also "against you."

Your Environment Is "Against" You

You, Brilliant Creator, spent the last 13-15 billion years (since you created the Big Bang), creating limitation.

You are the Grand Ninja Master at creating limitation.

Let's take "disease" for just one example:

You designed everything in your environment, including the people, and the systems—including the medical system.

Let's just say that one of your issues that you've been dealing with was a health or weight issue.

Do you know how many times in the last month—or 90 days—or a year, you've received information from the medical system (funneled through "other people") to remind you of that issue from the perspective of one of the lower four paradigms: What it is, what it means, the probable outcomes, etc...?

All of those reminders are you, from you and to you.

What if your issue was finding the perfect love partner?

Your painful childhood experiences created spells that convinced you that you just couldn't have the love you desire—unless it comes with pain.

And now, years later you're saying, "We'll, I'm going to dare to go for it again... I'm going to find the perfect love partner."

You turn on the radio and you hear a mourning, dying animal moaning, " I can't breathe—or live—because you have left me." Do you know how many times you'll get reminded of the end of love and the destruction of relationships? You are the radio station, the songs and the singer, all proving the rightness of your spells.

You literally designed the world with what many call "negative" jobs or a "negative" boss or a "negative" spouse, "negative" people, "toxic" people. We're not going to use that language anymore, but you know what I'm talking about.

Your environment is your biggest issue.

And if that weren't "bad enough"…

Your Mind is "Against" You

We covered this in the Fourth Key—the Spellbreaks section.

And now, we're going to go much deeper.

As we've established, your mind is designed to be the navigator of your life. It is perfectly suited for that job. The problem lies in the fact that, when we become triggered, we drop out of the driver's seat and the mind grabs the wheel to "keep us safe"—and that's when things go "wrong".

In every area of life where there is a spell in place, you have given the mind the steering wheel (and that is just about every area of life).

With the wheel in its less-than-capable hands, it drives according to your spells, rules, values, and paradigms—and they're going to come up to derail you every time you take a step towards what you actually want to experience.

In some ways, we could say that the mind is a partner of the brain, and the brain has spent millions of years thinking of really creative ways to not get eaten by tigers, and only a few hundred years in a mostly tiger-free environment. What's is the obvious outcome?

Remember there are only two choices—either you can be present (and focus on what you want to experience) or you can fall into thought.

When you are in a noisy, unconscious and addictive environment, it gets hard to "know" when you've fallen into thought. When you are triggered, you fall into thought. Suddenly you forget about living in conscious creation and your mind takes control, thinking about bills and kids and work and the 10,000 things that jump out at you in each moment to prove your spells "right".

When you can't see your mind's own blind-spots, it's like you're playing a rigged game. You can try to figure it out all you want—but freedom is not achieved through thought.

And then you start to think that you've done it again. You've invested more time, energy, money, or all 3 into a system that was supposed to work for you—but you're right back to where you were.

That familiar feeling of "what's wrong with me" starts to creep back in.

And then you see an ad for the next "self-help solution"...

Transformational Programs Are "Against" You

The odds are very high that you've been to one or more live events, or maybe just an evening of teaching. Maybe a money, business, or success course.

Maybe even a really great, feel-good, motivational seminar where you were even given some cool, transformational tools.

Be completely honest with yourself about what happened within 3 or 4 mornings of that last evening when you got home. It's even got a name. It's called Event Learning.

Studies have been done on attendees of transformational events and have shown quantitatively that each successive morning after they took that cab to the airport, got on the plane, walked in their front door, and got right back into their old environment (and paradigm), the effects of the event had dropped to nearly zero.

It may suck, but it is a fact.

Those events did not address the root, core issues, and you went home pretty much the same way you were when you left the house.

Summary

There is a lot of stuff against you.

And it is all you.

If you decide to "go for it", especially if you decide to go "all the way", you're going to face everything you have ever placed between yourself and what you want to experience.

It won't be easy. It won't always be fun.

It WILL be AWESOME!!!!

Secrets of a Conscious Creator: On Limitation

Q: Why would the universe bring in limitation?

Answer: Cuz it was bored! Blissing out and omm, omm, omm-ing for eons and eons! So It decided to create a different game! You can't have experience without limitation.

Have a question for me? See what others have asked and ask your own question at www.BreakYourSelfHelpAddiction.com/ama. I want to hear from you.

Chapter 10

The Universe Is Waiting—
Are You Coming?

"If you do not change direction, you may end up where you are heading."

—Lao Tzu

Reconnecting with the Universe

By now, you know that you are the driver of your life.

I would like to ask you a few pointed questions:

Can you imagine what life can really be like when you end the self-help loop and step into your Infinite Self?

What would it be like to join or co-create a community of people living in the Level 5 Paradigm?

Do you see and accept that your mind and old paradigms and spells have been running the show for long enough?

Do you see and accept that it is time—and that you have the ability—to take the wheel back into your own hands and direct your life to where you want it to go?

What might life be like if you make that choice?

To show you what is really possible, I'd like to invite one of my favorite clients and friends to share her story with you.

Joan's Story

Hi. My name is Joan Tremblay. I'm grateful Brian asked me to share my story. Like Brian, I'm going to be transparent with you.

I've been involved with personal development and self-help for the last 25 years. I'm an NLP expert, trainer and seminar leader. I've done many, many top-level programs, including Core Transformation and Core Energetics, most of Tony Robbins programs and more. I'm also a Hypnotist and have worked as a Hypnotism Instructor.

Frankly, I have tried, applied and even taught much of what is out there in the self-help and personal development world.

Today, I do corporate personal and professional development consulting and seminars.

25 years ago, I experienced a moment that prompted me to change my life.

During my childhood, I had experienced my mother's anger more than a few times, including being physically hit.

I had committed to myself that I would never be violent with my own children.

Then, when my son was one year old, he reached for something I had told him not to. I found myself grabbing his hand much more roughly and angrily than was necessary. Suddenly I made the sickening realization that I was perpetuating that same pattern. I decided, in that moment, that it was a must for me to deal with my anger issues.

So I dove into the personal development journey that would dominate my life for the next 25 years. To be clear, all of those programs had value.

Still, none of them really got to the depths I wanted to reach and none were as deeply rooted in spiritual truth as I wanted to go.

And so, all of these years later, I still had some deep personal issues I wanted to resolve, relating to relationships, self-love and money/business.

Well, about 6 months ago, I heard about an event going on at a friend's home where Brian was the speaker. It looked and sounded very interesting to me. I had just received some new insight into one of my core relationship issues and was hoping that I might get some further insight or transformation from the event.

At the time, I was also suffering from hip pain that had been there for years.

I really enjoyed Brian's unique energy and information, and when he called for a volunteer to experience a Spellbreak, my hand was up first.

There were about 30 or 40 people in attendance, but Brian was so calming and centered and created such a safe space, I was comfortable and able to really "go there" with him.

During the session, energy was shooting through my body, with hot and cold flashes moving through me and a lot of powerful sensations. I knew something different and significant was happening.

In about 15 minutes, it was over and my life-long relationship issue had completely dissolved. Brian asked me a few questions to see if there were any traces left, but it was gone.

I was kind of shocked to realize that the long-term hip pain, for which I had been taking medication daily, was gone. Completely gone. (6 months later, as I write this, it is still gone.)

The results were so amazing, I knew I wanted to work more with him. We did a few phone and video-call spell breaks and every single time, the issue I brought to him was gone. Completely gone. And every time, it stayed gone. Even more amazing, after every session, the next several days were filled with new energy, new insights and epiphanies.

Working with him was exactly what I was wanting.

So, when I found out that he was doing private retreats at his sanctuary in Hawaii, despite the investment, it was an easy "yes" for me. The biggest thing I wanted to address was that my money and business life seemed somewhat frozen and stagnant. Money had almost stopped flowing.

And I'm truly glad I made the decision I did. His retreat space in Hawaii is beautiful, comfortable, magical and filled with state of the art sound-healing, and therapeutic tools you just have to experience to believe.

On the first day, Brian had me start by writing out every issue I wanted to work through. After about an hour, I was amazed to find that I had 50, literally 50 issues on my page looking back at me.

We dove into Spellbreak after Spellbreak, and by the end of the first day, nearly everything on my list was gone. By gone, I mean they were non-issues for me. Brian has a way of dissolving the deepest roots of life-issues so they are just GONE—almost to the point that you can't remember what the problem was.

By the second day, every single issue on my list was handled. It's really unbelievable. And Brian makes it so easy, light, comfortable and fun, there is literally nothing that I feel uncomfortable exploring with him.

I'm thrilled to say that, just days after I left the retreat, I found that my next contract, which had been frozen, had been more than tripled. I'm making more money. I'm healthier. I'm happier. My relationships have never been better.

Two months later, everything is even better. I can give Brian the highest possible recommendation and I can tell you with certainty: Brian is a master at what he does. If you have one or more issues you want to deal with and you are really open and ready, Brian can help you.

Joan Jai Tremblay, 7/26/16

Joan is a joy to work with. So open and ready to break through the walls and so committed to the life of her dreams. I'm infinitely grateful for her and for the other clients from around the world who inspire me with their commitment to freedom.

GO DEEPER

If you'd like to see and hear Joan tell her story in her own beautiful voice, check out this short video: **www.BreakYourSelfHelpAddiction. com/joan.**

Why I REALLY Wrote This Book

I've been transparent and open with you throughout this book. I shared the deep, dark secrets of my past, all of the pains I went through, my self-help addiction, my homelessness and despair, and my huge breakthrough.

Next, I gave you the full "download" of the Level 5 Paradigm, as it has been given to me.

Then I gave you the 5 Keys to Freedom and I told you about the obstacles and opportunities you will likely face when you put this book down.

Now, I want to go even deeper into transparency with you. I want to tell you why I wrote this book.

I'm a selfish person. I embrace my reality as an Infinite Being of Light with access to Infinite Intelligence living in Infinite Possibilities. And I'm willing to focus on what I want to experience.

I desire to experience a world of true abundance and freedom—filled with love, joy and peace—for everyone who wants it, and specifically for myself and my children. I see things happening with the banks and global governments that are not as I prefer for them to be.

I see the growing seeds of tyranny in many countries and the uprisings in others. I see global meltdowns and I see—behind it all—the Global Awakening that you and I are called to be a part of...

Not to "fix" any "brokenness".

Not to "right" any "wrong".

Not to make "good" any "badness".

Nope.

Just to expand into more and more of what we want to experience.

I'm not interested in fighting or in being "against" anything, because that only creates more of the same.

When I had my breakthrough experience, I saw what was and is possible. And then, when I started to notice the flow of people coming to me for help with their spells, everything clicked for me. Almost every one of them had spent a lot of money on self-help and had gotten into being nearly—or fully—addicted to that cycle.

We are One. If I'm going to create the world I want to live in, I'm going to do it partially through my efforts to share this power, magic and freedom with my brothers and sisters who want it.

I realized that the Miracle Moment I had experienced, and the 5 Keys I had been given were worthless if I didn't put them into a form that enabled me to share them widely with all of my brothers and sisters who wanted to co-create, and live in, the same world of love and joy and peace that I am focused on.

I can deeply speak, from my soul, that I've done everything I can to make this book the most valuable and powerful tool for "transformation to liberation" for you.

I also know that I have left, by necessity, much of the power of my work out of this book.

If you and I were working together, I could literally spend a day or more helping you to get ALL of the power and magic out of EACH chapter in this book.

On top of that, there is no way for me to convey, in digital print, or on paper, the magic of a face-to-face Spellbreak, let alone a multi-day, Deep-Immersion Experience with me here in Hawaii.

Much deeper and closer to the heart, many of my clients tell me that the biggest benefit they derive from working with me arises from the "strange" fact that I live and emanate "Unconditional Love". There is no way I can give you the full experience of my intense love and caring for you through this written word.

So, I want to leave you with a word of encouragement and an offer of possibility.

If you have received what you wanted from this book and you feel "complete" regarding our time together, let me tell you: You CAN do this. You ARE the Infinite Source disguised as a person for the purpose of having experience.

If you're done, let me hear from you. I welcome your comments and feedback.

On the other hand, if you feel that all of this awesomeness is just the beginning, and that you've just begun, and that you want to go deeper—to jump fully off of the self-help train and onto the jet of awesomeness—to move from the "trap of transformation" to true liberation—I invite you to consider joining me for one of my "Transformation to Liberation" options—either online or here with me in Hawaii.

Thank you so much for all of your time, energy, attention and listening—and for your commitment to freedom.

I look forward to connecting and going even deeper into awesomeness with you.

With all of my love,

Brian

GO DEEPER

To take the next step with me, and learn more about my **Transformation to Liberation options.**

Check out **www.BreakYourSelfHelpAddiction.com/go-deeper**.

Acknowledgements

So-o-o many people contributed to the creation of this book. In fact, according to the paradigm I presented in the book, everyone alive, everyone who has ever lived, and everyone who is to come influenced this book.

Still, it is fitting for me to thank and mention those closest to me who either helped me to form the information or organize it into this form.

My mother, Joyce, and my father, Larry, helped to form me into this life and into the experiences that created this book and its teaching.

Jamie Moran and Alannah Avelin of Allvision Creative helped me immensely with fine-tuning the content and putting it into a comprehensible package. The brilliant Angela Lauria, of The Author Incubator, created the system that enabled me to harness my ideas and my "me-ness" and turn it into a book. Jade Rajbir Kaur's tireless, brilliant editing talents helped me organize and bring it all together.

Wayne Marshall, my Kaizen Brother, held down the fort for Level 5 Mentoring while I went underground for the writing.

Thank you all.

About the Author

Brian D. Ridgway is known to his clients as "The Spellbreaker". People who have experienced Brian's work have referred to him as a Shaman, Spiritual Teacher, and Healer.

A Speaker and #1 International Best-Selling Author, Brian helps people, mostly entrepreneurs and change-makers to step into the Conscious Creation of the body, health, business, wealth, relationships, life and world of their dreams.

After an abusive childhood leading to a life as a self-proclaimed Self-Help Junkie, Brian invested over $300,000 and tens of thousands of hours into his desperate quest for a life that "worked".

After nearly 30 years of intense research into religious, spiritual, self-help and personal development approaches, he abandoned his skepticism and dove into alternative approaches: energy work, Law of Attraction study and experimentation, belief-elimination, binaural brain-wave entrainment, meditation and "higher" spiritual approaches.

At the end of his rope, homeless and suicidal, in early 2011, he experienced his "Miracle Moment", and went from the idea of Infinite Possibilities to the experience of Infinite Possibilities. He was given the teaching that he calls, "The Level 5 Paradigm".

Brian teaches the Level 5 Paradigm and performs what he calls "Spellbreaks" in his programs, workshops and live events with private clients and with his audiences, online and off.

His ability to help people experience instant, deep and lasting breakthroughs is bringing him a rapidly expanding global following. Miracles and spontaneous healings are regular occurrences when Brian speaks.

Learn more or hire Brian at **www.BrianDRidgway.com**.

About Level 5 Mentoring

A Next-Generation Personal and Professional Development option for people who have already invested a great deal of time and/or money on their personal development but are still seeing the same results, Level 5 Mentoring offers change-makers, entrepreneurs and other purpose-driven people a powerful system of tools for creating the body, health, business, wealth, life and world of their dreams.

40 years of Research—Leading to One Powerful Solution
Founder Brian D. Ridgway has spent the better part of his life and over $300,000 in personal development investment to result in the Level 5 Paradigm, which he has been sharing professionally since late 2011. Thousands of people have experienced his work, with many reporting breakthroughs and even miracles. To learn more about Brian D. Ridgway and the Level 5 Mentoring Program, go to **www.BrianDRidgway.com**.

Transformation to Liberation Program

If you're like many people that Brian has worked with, you probably have some level of frustration with the world of self-help. The good news is that the time, energy and money you have spent on all those programs and coaches, books and events are not lost. The Transformation to Liberation program is designed to give you the next level of transformation that you've sought through personal development AND to liberate and accelerate the results you will see because of them. Brian works with clients on a 1-on-1 basis at the beautiful Sukhavati Retreat Center on the Big Island of Hawaii, offering multi-day private sessions, as well as through virtual 1-on-1 workshops over the course of 8 weeks. He also does year-long coaching through his Level 5 Mentoring program.

For more information on how to take part in the next Transformation to Liberation program, please visit **www. BrianDRidgway.com/go-deeper**.

Let's Keep Talking

This isn't the end, but rather the beginning.

Are you ready to take the next step?

In addition to everything else in this book, here is a "hidden gem" bonus:

You can access the Breath of Light Guided Experience, a unique life-and-mind shifting tool to help you Consciously Create your day and your life.

Just go here: http://breakyourselfhelpaddiction.com/BOL.

Contact Information:
Website: www.breakyourselfhelpaddiction.com
www.briandridgway.com
Facebook: www.facebook.com/brian.d.ridgway
Google+: https://plus.google.com/+BrianRidgway
Subscribe for more awesomeness: **www.youtube.com/c/ BrianDRidgway**

Morgan James
Speakers Group

We connect Morgan James published authors with live and online events and audiences whom will benefit from their expertise.

Morgan James makes all of our titles available
through the Library for All Charity Organization.

www.LibraryForAll.org

9 781683 504450